BEATDOWN: Three Plays by
JOSEPH JOMO PIERRE

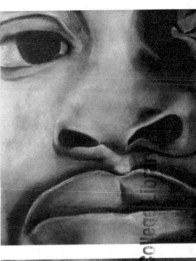
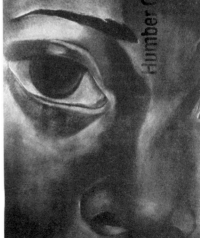

Born Ready | BeatDown | Pusha-Man

BEATDOWN:
Three Plays by
Joseph Jomo Pierre

Born Ready
a.k.a. Black on Both Sides

BeatDown
a.k.a. Life

Pusha-Man
a.k.a. The Seed

Playwrights Canada Press
Toronto • Canada

Playwrights Canada Press
The Canadian Drama Publisher
215 Spadina Avenue, Suite 230, Toronto, Ontario CANADA M5T 2C7
416-703-0013   fax 416-408-3402
orders@playwrightscanada.com • www.playwrightscanada.com

Financial support provided by the taxpayers of Canada and Ontario through the Canada Council for the Arts and the Department of Canadian Heritage through the Book Publishing Industry Development Programme, and the Ontario Arts Council.

Front cover design by JWAVE ART+DESIGN INC.
Production editing: JLArt

Library and Archives Canada Cataloguing in Publication

Pierre, Joseph Jomo, 1975-
      Beatdown : three plays / by Joseph Jomo Pierre.

"Born ready, a.k.a. Black on both sides ; Beatdown, a.k.a. Life ;
      Pusha-man, a.k.a The seed".

ISBN 0-88754-838-5

      I. Title.

PS8631.I475B42 2006   C812'.6   C2006-904054-0

First edition: July 2006.
Printed and bound by AGMV Marquis at Quebec, Canada.

*This book is dedicated to Cuthbert Pierre,
Christiana Ali and the entire Pierre family.
We all achieve as one.*

Table of Contents

INTRODUCTION

Honest. Raw. Compelling. Real. Really real. These were some of the words that came into my mind when I first picked up a copy of *BeatDown* in 2002. I had been given a copy of the play after it had been submitted to Cross Currents at the Factory Theatre, and while it was not included in that year's Festival, the power of the piece made it impossible for anyone to disregard. Thus began my association with Joseph Jomo Pierre.

I have had the good fortune to work on four plays that Joseph has written and I have been impressed with his fearless desire to confront issues head on. This desire is evident not only in the language he uses and the subjects he covers, but how he looks at these ideas with a fresh, clear view and a rigorous honesty.

He adheres to this honesty regardless of the fallout. Although he has always listened to thoughts and ideas about his plays he filters those comments through his own prism and will stand firm and committed to what he believes is the essential nature of his characters and his message.

When casting for the plays and workshops we saw many fine actors. And yet the casting was hugely difficult because it wasn't about "acting" the parts but about finding people who on some level had "lived" or "knew" those lives. It was that important to Joseph that there be a truth on as great a level with the actors as with the characters.

Joseph's work is unabashedly both male and Black. His writing reflects where he comes from and the attitudes of the people he has seen around him. They interweave themes of choice, growth, manhood, and responsibility.

Jayquese, Blackman, B-Side and Benjamin are all at that crucial point in their lives where the next decision will reverberate for years. And it is in these crux points where Joseph's plays live. *BeatDown*, where street life and fatherhood collide. *Born Ready*, where two men, they could have been brothers, meet over a gun called Peggy Sue. *Pusha-Man* where placebos meet our everyday needs.

Those are some interpretations of his plays. I have my own and I know that Joseph has his. But part of the joy of these works is that he allows, no, demands, that you bring your own interpretation to the plays. It's not about him telling you who or what Absolute really is, but that he has provided a canvas and you have to commit yourself and your understanding to create your own picture. I remember a radio interviewer trying three or four different ways to get Joseph to explain what *Pusha-Man* was about, and Joseph saying that he didn't talk about things like that and that the interviewer would have to see the show and work it out from her own view. I love that about this work. A synthesis of an idea developed on stage that expects and requires that the audience bring and give themselves to the work, or there will be no understanding.

So read and enjoy these plays. Find the wonderful music that Joseph has written. There are unique melodies within these lines. Tunes as poignant as a lullaby or as driving as any edge pounding out of a car's maxed-out stereo.

Philip Akin
Artistic Director
Obsidian Theatre
February 2006

Born Ready
a.k.a.
Black on Both Sides

l to r: Cara Ricketts, Joseph Jomo Pierre
photo by Aviva Armour-Ostroff

Born Ready a.k.a. Black on Both Sides was first produced at Theatre Passe Muraille, Toronto, in October 2005, with the following company:

Blackman   Joseph Pierre
B-Side   Mike G-yohannes
Peggy Sue   Cara Ricketts

Directed by Philip Akin
Stage Managed by Andrea Schurman
Set and Lighting Design by Trevor Schwellnus
Sound Music Coordinator: Nick Murray

l to r: Cara Ricketts, Mike G-yohannes
photo by Aviva Armour-Ostroff

CHARACTERS

BLACKMAN: Black male, late teens.

B-SIDE: Black male, late teens.

FEMALE/PEGGY SUE: Black female (mixed)

BORN READY

a.k.a.

BLACK ON BOTH SIDES

Lights come up as the DJ does a hectic drum-heavy mix.

Lights come up on the two Black men in silhouette. One holding a gun to the other's head.

Audio: Soundscape of a street. We hear an argument: "B-SIDE: Fuck you nigga. BLACKMAN: Fuck me? B-SIDE: Fuck you. BLACKMAN: Fuck me? Nahh, fuck you."

SFX: Loud, booming gun blast.

EFX: Blood spatters all over the projection at the back.

Lights go to black as the shot male falls to the ground in a slow motion effect. It's not revealed who is shot.

FEMALE/PEGGY SUE I am the official ride or die Bitch. The iconic, "Peggy Sue." Faithful to my man. Subservient to the fullest. Things I've seen, stories I've heard are never to be repeated. What goes down I'm suppose to take with me to the grave. But sometimes the lines get blurry. My vision like a cheap TV, all grainy. And all at once I can't differentiate who I'm riding for or why I'm riding at all… I loved him. *(pause)* Things I've seen, never to be repeated… but embraced by his sweaty palms. As if connected on some molecular level. I felt him, I heard him. He said he saw himself in his eyes. He said he heard himself in his voice. And if he coulda stopped time, or put his fingers on pause, he woulda asked him. What's his name where's he from. Stories never to be repeated. Fuck that!

FEMALE retreats.

SFX: Click click.

BLACKMAN and B-SIDE are revealed on the stage. Both men are dressed very similar. The street-type ghetto characters. It is important, however, that they do not acknowledge each other until their final encounter.

BLACKMAN *(sitting)* I'm from two large buildings, and four small ones. I'm from a small one-bedroom that neva faced the sun. We had a patch of grass in the middle. The grass was neva green. Matter of fact by mid summer that grass was just dirt.

B-SIDE   I'm from the hood. You know what a hood is? A hood is something that you pull over your head to conceal yourself. I'm from the hood where bricks and mortar conceal dead souls in living bodies.

FEMALE/PEGGY SUE   I know the beginning to every story, and often I'm a witness to the end. My own beginning…

BLACKMAN   When I was little, that patch of grass is where everything went down. I'd see the kids a little bigger than me playing stickball in the day. And the older folks huddled in the courts at night. Sometimes someone would walk across to the huddle, and they would laugh and give dap *(type of greeting eg. knocking of fists)*. And then the man would walk away. That's how they did it, that's how the deals went down. A little cream *(money)* for the green *(weed)*.

B-SIDE   We ran the inside of those buildings. We weren't allowed to leave our floor. But shit, we be kicking ball in the hall. Pitching marbles in those halls. That hall was our playground. Couldn't do that shit outside. Really the only time my little ass saw outside was when Ma Dukes took me.

FEMALE/PEGGY SUE   I can't tell you a touching story about my mother. Can't back it up with what it's like to be Daddy's little girl. For all I know, I am the true immaculate conception. Just came about, with a thought. Or maybe that's just my rationale for being motherless, for being fatherless. For neva knowing them.

>   *SFX: Heavy male voice: "You little fucks get outta here."*

B-SIDE   That mutha fuckka lived at the end of the hall. He was the one prick to wreck a youngins flex. A real loudmouth. He ain't have no kids or nothing. Matter of fact I don't think he ever left the building. Remember one time, one time Ricky got water guns. Ricky was that mutha fuckka that got everything first. There always a mutha fuckka like that. Shit we all poor, but that little shit always had everything. But that was my dog still.

FEMALE/PEGGY SUE   You could say I'm from a room surrounded by fresh faces whose stories are the exact same as mine. This orphanage. I'm too young and without the life experiences to give me a sense of identity. They say you are the sum of your experiences, that's what I've heard.

BLACKMAN   Moms was Trinidadian. A real beautiful woman. She neva took shit. My pops couldn't get away with shit around her. My mother was the type of woman that would skin a niggas dick if she got crossed. *(laughs)* I figure Pops enjoyed having skin on his cock, he ain't get on her wrong side too often. Don't think I eva seen him hit her. Don't get me wrong, that man was tough. He spoke with one of those heavy tongues. Like his word was bond. I seen my old man out on that patch of grass some nights. He be part of the huddle. Moms always had something on her mind. I was a little fuck, but I knew that she wasn't right. There was always something eating at her.

B-SIDE   So we playing water guns…

   SFX: "You little fucks."

And he starts his shit up again. I don't know if we wet his place up or whatever, but he was wildin.

   SFX: Door swings open.

Boom, his door slams. And there he is, this big Black fuck. He ain't got no shirt, no shoes, just his fuckin draws. That fucka looked like the devil. Boom, Bap, Boom, everyone dashed. But my bad little ass stood in the middle of the hall looking at him. *(using his hands to explain)* See where his door is at, the hall splits in two, one this way, one that way. So I figure he thought we all left. Boom, Bap, Boom, everyone took off.

   SFX: Ambulance.

FEMALE/PEGGY SUE   I am the sum of the countless men that have put their hands on me.

B-SIDE   But there I was, looking round the corner at him. Trevor's sista was only three she couldn't get away. I seen him pick her up and take her into his room.

BLACKMAN   Seven years old when my father died. *(pause)* His body face down in that patch of grass.

B-SIDE   People said he fucked her. I remember hearing his ass yelling that night. Somebody put a beating on his tail.

   SFX: "Pop, pop" gun shots.

BLACKMAN   Seven when whatever that was wrong with my mother killed her.

B-SIDE   And I saw his dead fuckin body carted out right in front of my door. Half his face missing.

FEMALE/PEGGY SUE   Bitches love to hate on each other. That's something you learn early on. I don't care how old they are hate is already running deep. They'll scorn you and hate you for things you have no control over. Because it was "my" fault that men showed me attention, right? I mean I had to be doing something to incite them, huh? See the jealousy is strong, even way back then; because we're all fighting for the same thing. Someone's affection. So each time a man came in and it was me he wanted to see, it was me he lifted and held… it was me the little girls were hating.

BLACKMAN   So basically my aunt raised me. But her building was a nightmare. I mean if Moms had hard times, my aunt had it worst. Sleeping in there was hell. First off, I had to share a room with my cousin. She was cool, but I useta have these real fuckin intense nightmares, and I always felt strange being weirded out in front of her. Then there was those fuckin demons. *(starts tapping his hands on the floor)* You hear that *(taps)* shhh, when the light go out, shhh, you hear them. *(He taps more. It sounds like little footsteps.)* Those fucks running ova your head. *(taps)* Back and forth like they fighting a damn war. Sounds like there is a million of them. Like any moment the ceiling will bust and they'll drop all ova my face. Then the walls start. *(taps)* I don't know how they learn to run sideways, but they start running on my walls. *(taps)* Just running like it's their fucking house. Like who the fuck was I, it's their crib. *(makes sound with his mouth)* Then I hear it. *(makes sound again)* Right under my bed. Like inches below my pillow I hear the shits talking to each other. *(makes sound)* And I hear them running… I'll come straight with you. I had some bitch in me when I was small. I useta go into my cousin's bed. She useta wrap her arms around me until I fell asleep. Wasn't shit sexual, you know. It was all, it was all just needing to feel safe.

FEMALE/PEGGY SUE   I guess it was from back then that I started to be a loner. I didn't care to socialize with girls, they didn't care to socialize with me…. It was men that would look at me excitedly and lovingly. That's where my first sense of being wanted came from. It came from a man's desire to have me. There'd be nights I'd pray that this desire would lead someone to take me away from there. Away from the envy.

B-SIDE   I ate Corn Flakes for breakfast. And sometimes Froot Loops for lunch. But Froot Loops was the jam though. Those shits was like candy. If I had my way, I would done with Froot Loops for dinner. *(laughs)* That's gangsta, sometimes I had Froot Loops for dinner. Sometime we had to add water to the juice so that it would last. Or put a slice of lemon or lime in a container of water. That was juice. You ain't know times. Unless you know about your ribs touching. About your ribs rubbing together when you breathe. Rubbing like a boy scout trying to make a fire. Your belly hurting cause you had plain rice covered in ketchup to eat. You ain't know times. You ain't have to beg Ricky to bring you a piece of chicken. Or stay playing at his house when it gets late, so his mom will feed you. And even that wasn't a given. Sometimes she send your little ass home, and you know the bitch know you ain't got no food at home. You ain't know times. Times is being eight and crying cause you poor. Times is when everyone you know and see is poor. Thas times! You come at me when you know times, when you know this.

BLACKMAN   A thirteen-year-old girl looking after me. Raising me. Keeping a house clean. Cooking, making sure I had something to eat. My aunt worked what seemed like 23 hours a day. I know it can't be that much, but it sure as hell felt that way. When I saw her it was always her back. It was always her walking out the door. So my cousin, she ain't had a life. It's partly cause of me you know. She couldn't be a young girl, she had to be a mommy to me. And she ain't ask for my Black ass, and all my problems to crash into her life. But all she ever did, was show me love. Thas all. I could say I ain't had shit. Well not a lot of shit. But I always had love.

FEMALE/PEGGY SUE   Steven. My white knight in Dockers and a cashmere sweater. He was the one that took me away from there. I guess he saw something worthwhile in taking care of a little Black girl, or something to that effect; you neva truly know a man's motives. But I sensed he was proud of me. Whenever guests would come over he'd make sure and bring me out for them to see. "Isn't she lovely" "Isn't she something" "She's beautiful." He seemed alright decent enough. But his touch was unsettling it was as if he didn't know how to hold me. There was something about me that caused fear to come to his eyes.

B-SIDE   I useta wonder why.

FEMALE/PEGGY SUE   He gave me up. I couldn't understand it, didn't know what I'd done. I guess when you come into this world abandoned its pretty asinine to expect anything else.

B-SIDE   Like this ain't no big time talk it's just a little kid thinking. But even then, even at them times I useta ask why. Like why I ain't ever had shit. Why things had to be so goddamn bad. I useta wonder if my mom did something to piss God off. I wondered if she was really bad when she was young. Who knows maybe she fucked my dad when she shouldn'ta. Maybe I was born in sin. Maybe it was all my grandmother's fault. She was a scary looking woman. I mean, she had a mustache, little hairs on her chin. I don't think my grandmother liked my little ass. I don't remember her hugging me or nothing. Okay, I know that ain't a bad thing the bitch was ugly. That was one ugly bitch. She looked like she was 200 years old. One of those original slaves, Kunte Kinte's mother or something. *(laughs)* Yeh, I'm tripping now. But I useta really ask why. I useta wonder if it would be like this every day of my life. If I would go through the same shit. If every day would be the same shit. I useta get sick to my stomach, like tasting the puke at the back of my mouth, just by thinking. All I know is I wanted to be grown up quick fast.

BLACKMAN   First time I seen breasts. I think I was in heaven. And I ain't even joking. I felt the bright lights, the warmth, all that shit. I was twelve, thirteen, and you know I was done fucking around with little girls, but that shit was nothing like seeing a woman's breast.

B-SIDE   Thirteen, that was a crazy year right there.

FEMALE/PEGGY SUE   He was kinda forceful.

BLACKMAN   Shit was crazy, off the hook. I think we musta been let out school early or something. Either way I was home earlier than usual. When I got home my cousin was in the shower, singing and shit. She was having a go at it, letting those notes out. I was in my room, our room, just laying down. And somehow, I don't know what was going on in my mind but somehow, I ain't notice when the shower stopped. *(deep breath)*

   SFX: Female voice singing.

She came out that door, not expecting anyone. Naked. Most of her body was dry, but I remember one breast had little drops of water on it still. She had these plumb brown breasts. These muthas were full. Double mouthful type tits. And they were firm, hardly moved. I had a fucking hard on, serious. I couldn't even make a sound to let her know that I was home. My eyes were fuckin glued to her boobs. Heart rate was off the chart. Thump, thump, thump, thump, thump. And Jesus if you could see her nipples. She had these chocolate nipples with perky tips. The tips pointed straight forward like bullets. I looked at her belly a little. Looked at her pussy for a quick sec. Didn't really see anything, the pussy was kinda hairy, plus the breasts were really what had me going. Of course later I grew to love pussy. *(laughs)* Well, I don't know if time stopped, it felt like it but I don't know. But when it started back again she was walking right towards the room. *(pause)* And that's when my erect penis began to pee. *(nervous laugh)* I started to wet myself I was so damn scared.

SFX: "Oh my God" followed by laughter.

And that's it. She just laughed like it was no big deal, came in the room, and asked me to leave so that she could dress. She neva teased me neva told my aunt nothing. Look, I neva felt anything sexual for her, but the first time I saw boobs, I saw me a nice pair.

FEMALE/PEGGY SUE   When he held me it was tight, a firm grasp. There was this possessiveness about him that turned me on. It was the fact that he made me feel like he had done it before, that he had control of the situation. Whenever he'd look at me there was this hunger. The dark of his eyes this violent jungle. I felt like he was as turned on by me as I was by his callous hands. He'd run those rough hands up and down my body. I was liking it. He dropped my skirt and started filling me up. Each time he'd put it in I'd get tighter and tighter, clenching until the last thrust. And when he put his finger in me it was too much. His whole body became rigid. His face contorted. And in one fleeting moment we both released, this euphoric release. He was my first.

Thick vapour, heavy smoke fills the room.

B-SIDE starts gutting a cigar, continues to turn it into a blunt.

B-SIDE   Where the weed came from. That was Ricky right there. I know nowadays it ain't nothing big for a thirteen-year-old to score weed. But when Ricky pulled that hook up, that was big shit. It was me, Ricky, two other dudes, inside the stairwell. Ricky was there trying to roll the shit, actin like he done it before. I know it was the niggas first time, well first time with weed. Knowing Ricky he probably practiced with some other shit, so that he could come out looking like a pro. Thinking back, he came with it, he came with it still. He rolled that shit pretty tight. There we was, nervous little fucks waiting for him to spark. *(takes a deep breath)*

BLACKMAN   (*continues with the deep breath*) I'm standing there naked. My body all shiny. My ass was all smooth like somebody shaved it. My balls were all smooth. My thighs were all sweaty, sticking to my balls. And he steps to me, pitchfork, horns, all that shit. But the bastard wasn't red. He was pitch black, tar black. So he reaches out and grabs my nuts, and starts pulling it. Tugging at my seeds. And like, as he's tugging I could feel these sharp blades cutting into my sac.

B-SIDE   When that scent it hit my nose. We became men. I remember how it just seemed to slide from my nose, down my throat. And that wasn't even my draw. It was Ricky's draw. When my hands were on that joint, all eyes were on me. Niggas were waiting to see if I choke or what. (*smiles*) It came natural, like breathing to me. I took that draw, held that shit in my mouth. Closed my eyes. (*exhales slowly*)

BLACKMAN   (*continues B-SIDE's exhale*) Warm blood flowing down my legs. At first just light drops, but it builds until a heavy thick flow rushes over my skin, and where my scrotum was, now feels like a huge empty hole. As if someone took a spoon and gutted out a grapefruit. My insides tickled by this warmth coming up my gutted-out hole. He grins at me, holding out my bloody crotch for me to see. I think I'm suppose to be in hell. But I wasn't feeling no pain. That was a high. That was some good herb, shit musta been "dro." (*type of weed, "hydro"*)

B-SIDE   I don't know why we sparked it on our floor. We shoulda known better than that. But true say, we weren't thinking about ramifications. We weren't thinking about getting caught. We was thinking about getting high. Plus we know not to go pass the 14th floor.

> *SFX: Hollow sound of steps coming up an apartment stairwell.*

Oh fuck! It's like we all let it out at the same time. Oh fuck. Niggas were all dizzy and shit, but we bolted up them stairs like we had all our senses. Musta been five flights later, and we standing silent. Ears all tuned in listening to see if we hear anything. Nothing. Whatever sent us blitzing was gone. But we were on the 18th fuckin floor, crack fuckin ally. So Ricky gets the damn idea from heaven that we should open the door and check it out. The two sheep they were all in for it. I wasn't really sure, that didn't seem like a good idea, especially when we was high. All that didn't matter though. Before we could make a move, my eyes caught something, just hanging over a step. I was more excited more than scared. I blocked out everyone and just started walking towards it. I picked it up. Picked it up and put it under my shirt. I picked up food, no more starving. I picked up clothes, no more dressing poor. I picked up hope. I picked up somebody's dashed away burner. Even Ricky's mouth dropped. I beat him to this one. (*motions with his hands*)

> *SFX: "Click, click." The sound of pulling back on a gun.*

BLACKMAN   I still don't understand when she met him. I mean when did she have time? It wasn't like she was social and stuff. Couldn't find her at a club even if you tried hard. She didn't love him, I can't see it being love. Nahh, nahh, nahh, there's no way it was love. There's no way she could get caught up in some dude's slick words. She was built betta than that.

B-SIDE   Didn't start shaving till I was sixteen, was kinda late with growing the whiskas. Shaved them that night though. We were gonna hit this all-ages jam, the squad was like eight, nine deep. Around then we always rolled heavy like that. Felt powerful. Ricky was all sour. I mean he was my dog but I didn't know how to find out what was busting a nigga's weiny. To me some hip-hop, some reggae, grinding on some chicky-poo's ass woulda put a nigga at ease. Wrong recipe for the wrong night.

BLACKMAN   You ever walk into a room, and your first notion is to get the fuck outta there? I don't believe in spirits and shit but there's this weird thing that happens; you get feelings and stuff. My problem is why you get them when you open the door? Why the fuck don't you get them before? Makes sense to me, if I was the man handing out feelings and notions and shit I'd hand them out before. 'Cause when you open the door you just stepped into shit, and if you run out you still got shit on your foot. And when shit's on your foot you stuck with that smell. *(pause)* I open the door, and here come feelings, and notions and shit. There is this dude sitting on the couch next to my aunt. Wasn't nothing truly distinctive about him. He looked pretty much like any other nigga. That being said he could've been just as trifling. He gives me one of those smiley nods like he knows me. Like we spose to be friends. But I don't know dude. And I don't know why he's flashing them yellow-ass teeth. Plus ain't nobody wearing FUBU no more. He needs to take them shits back. *(pause)* Okay, I smiled back at him, it was fake as shit but I smiled back at him. And my teeth were white.

B-SIDE   By the speaker was this, light skin-ed thing with blonde hair. Parasuco jeans, the top of her thongs showing. She was with these two fat chicks; well one was fat the other was just thick. Hmmm, fuck being technical they was fat. Pretty girls always walk with body guards. *(smiles)* Maybe it makes them look more pretty. Maybe that's why I thought she was hot. Maybe it was just cause she was light skin-ed. Maybe it was seeing the thongs. But she was definite fire I know that much. Hormones did what they were suppose to do; made me step to her. Your boy was geared to the till, white gold, a clean pair of ones. *(Nike Air Force 1's)* I grind on that thing all night. Grind so hard that I could feel her pubic bone. Angled my body so that I could feel myself grinding between her lips. The night coulda ended right there.

BLACKMAN   I knew that sitting on that couch wasn't where I wanted to be. Yep, came to that answer real fast. So I just made my way to my room. *(pause)* When a woman cries don't it feel so…. There's my cousin sitting on the side of the bed crying. My head starts hurting me. Nobody's said anything but I know this ain't good for me. Felt just like when Moms died. Head starts pounding. She's holding me, and her wet cheeks are pressed on my cheeks. And she's scared. I don't think they saw her crying, I mighta been the only one she let see. She got a suitcase packed with her clothes and I find out she got a baby in her belly. Guess she gotta be a mommy all ova again. I guess yellow teeth got a reason to be smiling and nodding. She says she loves me, and that I betta behave and be there for my aunt. I tell her I'd kill him if he ever hurt her. She laughs. He's 6'2" 220. She laughs.

B-SIDE   Last song comes on, the regular slow shit. I had my share of dancing so I was chatting it up making sure I had her number and everything correct. Ricky comes up and grabs her hand. She ain't know him so she pulls away. I mean that's my boy so I ain't really care, so I let her know that it's okay. He grabs her again real aggressive like. Hun pulls away again. Boom! Ricky gets all jacked up calling her a bitch and shit. I'm tryna calm him down, and he starts yellin shit at me.

SFX: "You think you the fucking man now."

I'm not sure what he's saying but he's real pissed off. Boom I'm draped against the speaker his hands round my neck. I catch chicky-poo's eyes, she's like "what the fuck." I'm looking at my best friend and I swear he's tryna kill me. It was like slow motion, I'm almost choked and without thinking I manage to draw my piece. I got my gun pressed to my best friend's rib. His eyes are daring me to shoot. He can see in my eyes if his hold doesn't loosen up I will. *(pause)* It wasn't about no bitch, we weren't like that. It was about a shitload of things that only Ricky knows about. *(pause)* There was no shooting. He walked away. I knew right then life had changed.

BLACKMAN   There's girls that turn into women right in front of you. There's panties you want to get into. But that shit's drastic. It ain't as simple as when I seen my first boobs. Now you just wanna lose yourself in that woman. You just wanna hide yourself in her. I be planting my face between those tits, pulling them into my cheeks. That's like one of the most peaceful places I've found. In my mind I'm just a youth again. She can't tell, she just thinking I'm loving that tit. She don't know that a nigga is just hiding. But once you on the breast you know draws gone drop. And when the draws drop that's a whole new situation to handle. You wanting the sex, you wanting that warmth, but you sure as fuck ain't wanting no kid. Before you pull out the chef you know your excuse gonna be, the kid ain't mine.

B-SIDE   That shit ain't mine. Don't come to me tryna parlay some dudes pickney. I mean, yeh I'm gonna be out there tryna get me some; just don't throw no added stress on me. That's why I be messing with the wild chicks, give me a sket any day. It sounds fucked up, but at least with a sket you know she ain't tryna see no kid either. You just flippin them, rotatin em, a different beat every night. I'm not tryna be a bastard about it, but sometimes the weed don't work.

Sometimes the rum don't work, sometimes the only place to escape this everyday bullshit is between some chicky poo's thighs.

FEMALE/PEGGY SUE   When do you know a man's soul? When do you see a man's soul? You see a man's soul on a Tuesday.

BLACKMAN   Things just aren't all that simple no more. It ain't about people tryna feed you. You gotta feed yourself, you gotta feed them. See you a man in this world now. Yeh, sometimes you still feel like youse a child; but you got some height on, you got some age on you. And those seem to be the only qualifications needed. I wasn't one of those motherfuckers tryna rush into being a man. I ain't never seen nothing glamorous about what my father went through. Nothing glamorous about what my mother done been through, to make me want that. But all the weed in the fuckin world can't keep you away from the truth. Some point during those 24 hours in the day you gonna find yourself stuck in the middle of reality. Things ain't gonna be like they was.

> *FEMALE stands over B-SIDE who is sitting at a table. A gun is on the table.*

FEMALE/PEGGY SUE   You see a man's soul at 3am on a Tuesday. When the TV's off, sometimes one lit candle, the scent of cigaweed, a glass of SunnyD. That's when you see a man's soul. It's not when he's loud and boisterous. It's not when he's running crew deep. Dem times it's their energy that fuels him. Dem times he can fall back to the shadows. You see his soul when he can't sleep, when there is no one but you and him. When his face is either buried in the palms of his hands, or sunken into the table. I've seen him, in silence, biting on his bottom lip, crying. The stillest thing just crying—

> *B-SIDE gets up and turns towards PEGGY SUE. During these next few sequences she goes between doing her monologue and interacting.*

B-SIDE   *(to PEGGY SUE)* I need to get far away from your ass.

FEMALE/PEGGY SUE   What? Wait, slow down. I didn't do anything.

B-SIDE   You don't understand what you do to me.

FEMALE/PEGGY SUE   What do I do, besides day in day out being there for you?

B-SIDE   You make me complete. I hold you and I feel like I can conquer the world. Do you know what that feeling is? Do you know what that feeling is? That's a dangerous thing.

FEMALE/PEGGY SUE   I'm not following you, how is that dangerous? Isn't that what I'm spose to do?

B-SIDE   Listen, its breaking me up, tearing me, up. I know I'ma be vulnerable without you; half the man I am without you—

FEMALE/PEGGY SUE   So fuck it then. You make me complete, I make you complete, what's the problem?

B-SIDE   Don't you see my eyes sometimes. When I'm holding you, you ever rest on my eyes?

FEMALE/PEGGY SUE   *(pause)* No... I... no... *(monologue)* He told me I was the only thing he had. The only thing he could put his life on was me. He said he ain't know what to make of his situation, but he knew how it would end. He dropped those heavy eyes on me and told me he knew how it would end. And I knew what he meant, we'd both seen it all before.

B-SIDE   You and I, if we stick together I can see it all.

FEMALE/PEGGY SUE   I'm not leaving your side. I'll keep pulling you and pulling you back.

B-SIDE   What do you want? Do you want my blood running down some drain? You wanna be there when my temper gets me in some shit and I—

FEMALE/PEGGY SUE   Of course not. That's why I'm with you. To keep that from happening.

B-SIDE   Are you willing to kill for me—?

FEMALE/PEGGY SUE   YES!! *(silence)*

> *B-SIDE shakes his head and turns his back.*

(monologue) Goodbyes can be just as unnerving as the first hello. Especially the goodbye from someone you know loves you. Held you like a prized possession. But he said that as long as I was a part of his life, as long as I was there as a crutch, his ending would be set in stone. He was leaving me because he didn't want blood on our hands. I didn't want blood on his hands either, I'd seen his soul. And if for that soul to flourish I had to go, I wished neva to see him again.

B-SIDE   Gone are the days of riding the train after school with your boys, looking for someone your size to boost. Flashing your chrome if you need to. You doing dirt, but you bonding with your boys. You doing dirt with your fam. You gaining war stories to look back on, laugh on. And if you make enough noise, word gets on the streets about your crew. Then you really living the life. You sipping that ghetto fabulous juice. To two hundred or so people you are actually the shit. And I wished it woulda just stayed like that. Just about fam, just about jokes. But that all changes. All the shit just gets to the point where it's more complicated. And a nigga gotta live up to the hype. Now you boosting a store, or finding out who boosting a store. You wearing Jordan nineteens *(Nike Air Jordan XIX)* before Jordan knows the shitz out, more gold on your body than you got dollars in the bank. More flash more bitches.

FEMALE/PEGGY SUE   And as soon as you think you're out of this shit; it's nighttime and you find yourself in some other man's hands.

BLACKMAN faces in the direction of PEGGY SUE during this.

BLACKMAN   *(to PEGGY SUE)* Do I hold you the way they held you? Do I make you feel the way they made you feel? A waste of questions huh? You're just gonna tell me what you think I want to hear. Shit I know the routine.

FEMALE/PEGGY SUE   And his touch is that same as the one you ran from. And he holds you with the same depth of commitment.

BLACKMAN   *(to PEGGY SUE)* You know why I mess with you? I mess with you because I know when I die you'll be right by my side. Sounds like some Romeo and Juliet shit huh. But it ain't like that, I ain't tryna take my own life.

FEMALE/PEGGY SUE   He also got dreams, bigger dreams than you think.

BLACKMAN   *(to PEGGY SUE)* I'm tired of getting migraines thinking of a way out this shit. What's the Black man's hustle bebe? Everybody got a hustle what's ours?

FEMALE/PEGGY SUE   And you're there laying on his lap, and you wish you could look up and give him all the answers he needs. Cause every day that he's breathing is a day that you're loved. Every day that his blood doesn't escape from that tissue is a day you don't have to cry.

BLACKMAN   You can't break out of the world you in. You can't keep your mind intact. Start thinking about how you look, how you dress. Start worrying that you getting left behind, that she ain't gonna want your broke ass. Neva a second, where you ain't thinking where the next dollar coming from. It's like a battle everyday. You battle today for tomorrow, you battle tomorrow for the next day. And through it you neva happy. How can you be happy when you focus on battling. And the stress is a mutha fucker. The stress, drives a nigga to weed. The stress drives a nigga to fucking with wild bitches. The stress sits you down, and pours a forty down your throat. The stress makes you not give a fuck cause you not happy anyway.

FEMALE/PEGGY SUE is face-to-face with BLACKMAN

FEMALE/PEGGY SUE   I can't believe I believed I could hold on to a dream. I can't believe I believed I could sidestep my past. Somehow I believed I could be safe with you. But my stupidity is in believing you'd be safe with me.

B-SIDE   This life, this world, everything is frantic. The pace is frantic. I'm hustling, scooping off the top so I can have the clothes, the jewels. But it's not an easy thing having a little something around a bunch a people who ain't got nothing. You know their eyes be big. Big empty pools of wanting. And you know their hearts are all black. No longer knowing how to love or care, just bruised and angry. But knowing that they are all envious, well that shit just fuels you more. That makes you the man on some shallow level. But sometimes it don't matter what that level is, what matters is that you're the man.

SFX: "You're the man."

You're the man cause bitches wanna bed with you. You're the man cause niggas wanna hang with you. And it's frantic, the whole life it's all frantic. Nothing's slow, nothing's steady. Shit just seem to tumble into each other. No long straight roads. Just a bunch a quick corners. Your head always snapping, this way, that way. You're the man cause you got a burner. And you ain't scared to use her. That's why you're the man.

BLACKMAN   It's like no matter what, you still that dude cuddled up with his cousin. You still that grown ass man that can hear the rats running. But you know more things, seen more things.

FEMALE/PEGGY SUE   Maybe I shoulda jammed. There's a chance he woulda stayed home.

B-SIDE   When everything your whole life been so hard to get. When you struggle just to eat just to stay warm. There comes a time where you ain't wanna struggle for shit. You just want things to come easy.

SFX: Sound of the rats running.

BLACKMAN   But all that you know, *(smiles)* all that shit you done been through, can't change one thing. Your life ain't worth no more than it did when you were born.

FEMALE/PEGGY SUE   Maybe I shoulda told him I knew how it would end. I coulda detailed his life.

B-SIDE   You gotta pull. Every day you gotta be ready to pull. Cause that's the new rule, the new law you gotta live by. You either live by the trigger or the prayer. Fuck a prayer!

FEMALE/PEGGY SUE   Our stories are never meant to be retold. But there's been too much blood on my name. Too much pain I can't express. Too many times I've been silent while the hand of one lover grasped me, while ushering the end to another. So fuck it!!! If I can't run from their touch let them run from mine.

> *BLACK MAN and B-SIDE have an altercation. The murder/jacking unfolds in real time. Violence unfolds as FEMALE/PEGGY SUE details the event. BLACKMAN ends up killing B-SIDE.*

FEMALE/PEGGY SUE   It started with two guns.
One black and one chrome.
A Glock and a Ruger.
2 clips checked twice to make sure that they full.
Safetys' off, gotta make sure them safetys' off.
Placed in the waists of sizes 38, 34.
Probably a couple sizes too big for the frame they on.
There's a motherfucker here,

And over there something about somebody's mother cunt.
There's a fuck you, and a fuck you,
What you gonna do, and what you gonna do,
Yeh nigga, what nigga.
And they chest start heaving,
And the blood start pumping,
And they eyes get red,
Cause the anger's breathing.
Somebody gets pushed,
Somebody pushes back.
Somebody gets bitch slapped,
Now you know a nigga ain't having that.
So the fingers become fists,
And the bones be bricks.
Blowweeee!!
There's a tremor in his body,
As his flesh vibrates.
Powww!!
There's an elbow in the rib,
As the spine rotates.
Poww!! Pow! Poww!!
Combination of blows,
Roy Jones in they veins.
But he ain't backin down,
And he ain't backin down,
So a leg is raised
And a foot connects,
So a leg is raised again,
But this time it's snatched,
And a nigga falls back,
Right flat on his back.
But that pavement ain't so soft,
It ain't so forgiving.
You know that shit ain't so soft,
That shit ain't so forgiving.
So he grits his teeth,
And he curls his lips,
His nostrils flare,
Those broad Black nostrils flare,
And he's sucking, sucking, sucking,
Gasping for air.
Cause who's this motherfucker really thinks he is,
That I'll be bitched in these streets like this.
Disrespected in my own fuckin streets like this!
That's what he's thinking.

So I'm drawn,
Shit I'm looking pretty in the light.
The sudden power,
Revitalizes his body,
And he springs to his feet.
You ain't so fucking bad now huh?
All that tuff shit, where all that tuff fucking shit at now huh?
"Fuck you nigga, fuck you!"
Fuck me? Fuck me? Nahh fuck you!
And as they fucks collide,
He sees something in that other nigga's eye.
Something resonates,
But he can't finger it.
There's something in that nigga's eye.
There's a flash of a hand,
To the pocket with the Glock.
So I'm forced,
To the temple of a dome.
There's something in that nigga's eye.
He really doesn't know what started this shit,
Or what it was that escalated this shit.
Why the two-tone chrome had to leave his hip.
Something.
He's caught in the middle of a thought,
By a hand that's too impatient to wait.
The same hand that reached for the Glock,
Once again tests its faith.
Placcca!!!
I deliver his faith.
It's called learnt reaction,
Or muscle memory.
Placca!!!
He said he saw himself in his eyes,
He said he heard himself in his voice,
And if he coulda stopped time,
Or put his fingers on pause,
He woulda asked him,
What's his name? Where's he from?
But there's no stopping this time.
There's no pause in this life.
And though that nigga's every movement was his,
Instinctual reactions that only living his life coulda bring,
He said he musta been crazy,
He said it just couldn't be.
That nigga had a different mother,

That nigga had a different father,
That nigga was a couple of shades different,
That nigga couldn'ta been me.
He's convincing himself,
That nigga couldn'ta been me.
But I know that nigga's eyes.
I've felt that nigga's touch.
I've seen that nigga's soul.
Yeh, yeh, yeh,
Different mother, different father, different shade.
But,
He was you.
Suicide it's a suicide.

The end.

BeatDown
a.k.a.
Life

CHARACTERS

JAYQUESE: Black male, early twenties. Drug slinger.

TRINI: Black male, early twenties, West Indian. Drug slinger. Talks in his Trinidadian accent.

TUPAC: Black male, early twenties. Drug slinger. Total American culture thief.

JEROME: Black male, early twenties. Been on the streets the longest. Large male, drug slinger. Takes what he does seriously.

TERINA: Black female, early twenties. University student.

TASHA: White female, early twenties. A dancer. Wealthy family.

CINDY: Black female, early twenties. Life done fucked her up.

LEXUS: Black female, twenties. Hooker.

PLAYWRIGHT'S NOTES

This play takes place on one night. Jayquese finds out that he is about to be a father, then seeks to escape this news by visiting first with the women in the play and then with his boys. The action unfolds on any urban street where life and death occurs. The BeatDowns throughout the play are brief snippets of Jayquese's ongoing nightmare. Keep the action flowing and keep the actors RAW. Let's do this muthafaka right.

BEATDOWN

a.k.a.

LIFE

SCENE ONE

BEATDOWN #1

Projection comes up. It is the POV (point of view) of a child walking down a dark hallway. We hear the muffled sound of the child saying "Daddy" on the audio. The projection goes to black. Lights come up on the stage. It's nighttime. JAYQUESE snaps his head looking in the direction of the sound. Seeing nothing he continues to walk on.

JAYQUESE   You walk these crazy streets and you see these neon lights. You breathe this air every day, every night. You wonder if you givin life to the city or the chaos givin life to you. You walkin beating your $100 dollar soles on the eyes of the world. See them pavements done seen everything life has to offer. That's why cement so strong, it done seen it all. And you walkin, you leavin footprints. FOOTPRINTS. I useta have this plaque. This story about footprints in the sand…. "One night a man had a dream. He dreamed he was walking along the beach with the Lord. Across the sky flashed scenes from his life. For each scene, he noticed two sets of footprints in the sand, one belonging to him, the other to the Lord. When the last scene flashed before him, he looked back at the footprints in the sand. He noticed that many times along the path of his life there was only one set of footprints. He also noticed that it happened at the very lowest and saddest times in his life. This really bothered him… naw more like fucked him up, so he questioned the Lord about it. "Lord, you said that once I decided to follow you, you'd walk with me all the way. But I noticed that during the most troublesome times in my life there is only one set of footprints. I don't understand why when I needed you most, you would leave me." The Lord replied, "My precious, precious child, I love you and I would never leave you. During your times of trial and suffering, when you see only one set of footprints in the sand IT WAS THERE THAT I CARRIED YOU." …It was there that He carried you. Now that's some deep shit. Sometimes I be looking back over my shoulders, X-ray visioning that cement. And I ain't seeing no footprints, not even my own.

Walking towards him is LEXUS dressed like a lower-end hooker. JAYQUESE's back is turned away from her.

LEXUS   A hit for a suck. Come on, you ain't never had your cock waxed the way I can wax it.

JAYQUESE *(to himself)* Oh shit. *(JAYQUESE turns around to look at LEXUS.)*

LEXUS Oh shit! *(Taken aback that it's JAYQUESE, she starts walking away in haste.)*

JAYQUESE Where you going? *(She keeps walking.)* Girl you betta stop walking. Lex!

> *Hearing her name come from his mouth, she cautiously turns to face him.*

Get your tail over here.

LEXUS I'm not coming over there.

JAYQUESE You not coming over here? I haven't seen you in weeks and you just gonna up and run away when you notice me. What we ain't fam? We ain't peoples no more?

LEXUS It's not even that.

JAYQUESE Why don't you come over here?

LEXUS Why don't you come over here?

JAYQUESE *(laughs)* Aight, I'm coming over there. *(JAYQUESE walks over to her.)*

LEXUS Mmm, you still looking sexy, Jay.

JAYQUESE I'm looking good?

LEXUS Yeh, I'd suck your dick for free. *(reaches for his crotch)*

JAYQUESE I thought I told you about that kinda talk.

LEXUS Yeh, I know, you tell me about a lot of things, Jay. I just wished that you'd sell to me like you useta.

JAYQUESE Things changed Lex. You useta pay, wasn't about sucking no nigga's dick. This went from recreational to a full time job for you.

LEXUS Yeh, things changed, Jay. They changed. You ain't really know how they changed.

JAYQUESE Man you bigger and brighter than this, Lex. I don't think you know how niggas was sweating you in school. You was the thing.

LEXUS I was?

JAYQUESE Damn yeh.

LEXUS You was sweating me?

JAYQUESE Putting me in a corner now?

LEXUS Come on... were you?

JAYQUESE *(smiles)* Back then you was that older girl that a little nigga could only dream of being with. I was sweating you crazy bad.

LEXUS Not any more? *(pause)*

JAYQUESE Lex, you need to be cleaning yourself up.

LEXUS You know it's hard.

JAYQUESE I know, that's why I told you I don't wanna see you out here pregnant and all of that.

LEXUS I'm trying.

JAYQUESE You had the baby?

LEXUS A girl.

JAYQUESE Goddamn, you had a baby girl? What's her name?

LEXUS Hope. *(nervous giggle)*

JAYQUESE Hope. Look Lex, you need to start doing things for your baby. You got a beautiful body don't let niggas abuse it.

LEXUS Maybe all I need is a man like you.

JAYQUESE Naw, cut your tongue there, certainly not like me.

LEXUS I could handle one like you, your height everything.

JAYQUESE Tryin to sweet talk me.

LEXUS Nigga please.

JAYQUESE Look at me. Lexus look at me. I'ma break you off some cash. But I don't want you to be goin to the next man with my money, you hear me. You take this here and buy your daughter some diapers. Look, this here is for you, buy yourself some Victoria Secrets; feel sexy.

LEXUS Look at you, my sweet Gabriel.

JAYQUESE Gabriel?

LEXUS You a beautiful man Jayquese. Beautiful.

JAYQUESE I don't know about all that, but get yourself cleaned up… and give your daughter a hug for me.

LEXUS You know you can still have that offer.

JAYQUESE What offer?

LEXUS You know, for free.

JAYQUESE LEX!

LEXUS I'm going, off the streets right? *(She walks away.)*

JAYQUESE   Right.

LEXUS   *(fading out of sight)* A HIT FOR A SUCK.

> *Lights go to black and come up on the BeatDown.*

BEATDOWN #2

BeatDown projected on a screen.

Audio: Sound of a record played backward (scratch).

Dream sequence, continuation of the previous. The child takes a few steps until he is pushed. This thrust sends him over an edge and he is in the midst of a freefall. POV of him falling down a black bottomless hole (imagine jumping off the moon). Cut to a child in bed having a nightmare—his face contorted. Black.

SCENE TWO

> *Lights come up on the boys. The boys are huddled together while TUPAC is off on his own going over some lyrics. The group should be silent while TUPAC does his thing.*

TUPAC   I got a pen and a pad
Two eyes and two ears
But they act like I'm taliban
Niggas get more dissension/than Osuma and his henchmen
Fuck it, we ain't fly them planes!
Yeh
Amount of blood you done shed
Hate you done bred
System that keeps fucking the poor
Niggas carrying weight/from state to state
They minds on movin that raw
Man,
Fuck a reparations
We only seen lynchins
I'ma let you know what's in store
When them Muslims start firing/there ain't no back tracking
We might not wanna fight your war!
Wow

> *TUPAC starts to walk over to the boys, as he does so the lights fade to black.*

…Just my pen and my pad.
Just a pen just a pad…

Lights go to black.

SCENE THREE

Lights come up on TASHA's bedroom. JAYQUESE is under the sheets in a way that would indicate that he's giving her head.

TASHA   *(giggles)* Don't stop. Little Miss Muffet sat on a tuffet eating her curds…

JAYQUESE   *(sticks his head out from under the sheets)* What are you doing?

TASHA   Jay come on, go back down.

JAYQUESE   What the fuck's this Muffet shit?

TASHA   Jay you're killing the sensation, go, go back down.

JAYQUESE   I do you right?

TASHA   Yes Jay you do me right.

> *JAYQUESE kisses her on the neck and works his way back under the sheet.*

Ahh! You know you're like a bloody snake. *(giggles)* Oou! Little Miss Muffet sat on a tuffet… *(He bites her.)* OOUCH!

JAYQUESE   I thought I told you to stop that kiddie shit.

TASHA   You didn't have to bite me…

JAYQUESE   You didn't have to Little Miss Muffet.

TASHA   You're no fun.

JAYQUESE   Fine, I'll put the tongue away for the rest of the night.

TASHA   Jaaay.

JAYQUESE   What?

TASHA   Get the whipped cream and go back.

JAYQUESE   Don't you think I've brought it on long enough?

TASHA   NO!

JAYQUESE   Why you such a fiend for what I got?

TASHA   I like the things you do.

JAYQUESE   I get my freaks on?

TASHA   Yes, yes you do. You are good with your hands, lips, good with your hips.

JAYQUESE   And you're no chump with your hips, your thighs, eyes, the small of your back.

TASHA   The small of my back. I like that one.

JAYQUESE   Tash you know you keep getting sexier and sexier.

TASHA   I do?

JAYQUESE   No doubt. Lemme look at you.

TASHA   Okay, look.

JAYQUESE   Yo! Smile, do your lips like this, LL COOL J style. No doubt, you're sexy. You building up some muscles too.

TASHA   It's all that dancing. I feel like my calves are ready to fall off.

JAYQUESE   Officially you wouldn't be sexy anymore.

TASHA   If I didn't have calves, I wouldn't be sexy?

JAYQUESE   Fuck no. Then you wouldn't be sexy in heels no more. And I love you in heels.

TASHA   That's pretty insensitive.

JAYQUESE   Ohh, that word again.

TASHA   Yeh.

JAYQUESE   Tasha, If I had no fuckin ass would I be sexy?

TASHA   Who said you're sexy now?

JAYQUESE   For real.

TASHA   Yes Jay, to me you'd still be sexy.

JAYQUESE   That's major league Bullshit. Why you girls gotta be like that, all lying with that romantic crap. I know I'd look fucked without an ass.

TASHA   You're missing the point?

JAYQUESE   Missuss, what's the point?

TASHA   The point is that the complete you is more important than any one part.

JAYQUESE   But an assss, is an essential part to the overall structure. A man with no knowledge of his assss has no knowledge of his heaaad.

TASHA   Now I know what your problem is.

JAYQUESE   Ooohh! You tryna kill me. Ummm, you tryna kill me. *(kisses her)*

TASHA   You don't think I'd look sexy with no calves? *(pulls sheet to cover more of her body)*

JAYQUESE   Well, I guess you'd still look sexy, I mean your boobisms are ample compensation. *(pulls sheet back down)*

TASHA   Slick really is a Black man.

JAYQUESE   And vanilla don't be tasting that bad.

TASHA   Why are you calling me vanilla?

JAYQUESE   Cause you're WHITE! *(They both laugh.)*

TASHA   I don't taste too bad?

JAYQUESE   Tash… no, no baby.

TASHA   Jay, how about I come see you tomorrow?

JAYQUESE   I'm busy. I'll come and check you later in the day though.

TASHA   I know you're not busy. It's not like you're working 9 to 5.

JAYQUESE   Don't rag me Tash. I'ma check you later.

TASHA   If I'm not around do you think of me?

JAYQUESE   Yeh.

TASHA   Yeh…. You know a lot of people won't understand what we have.

JAYQUESE   Are you understanding?

TASHA   I AM A GROWN WOMAN.

JAYQUESE   So?

TASHA   So, I do what I want. My judgement is the final one, no matter what anyone thinks.

JAYQUESE   Girl we're better off when we just avoid this here.

TASHA   For how long?

JAYQUESE   As long as we're together.

TASHA   I'm going to New York next week. *(pause)*

JAYQUESE   Ohh.

TASHA   We got invited to dance in this festival. I'm going to be away for two weeks.

JAYQUESE   And you just heard that?

TASHA   No.

JAYQUESE   So what kept you from letting out the news?

TASHA   You need a notice to organize my replacement?

JAYQUESE   You know I don't need notice for shit.

TASHA   That's not the point. The point is we need to clarify some things so that I can leave with a peace of mind.

JAYQUESE   Clarification, I dig you, you dig me, the sex is hot butter.

TASHA   And that's it?

JAYQUESE   I don't know maybe there's more shit.

TASHA   FUCK YOU!

JAYQUESE   Tash you just cussed.

TASHA   I don't give a fuck.

JAYQUESE   Baby that shit don't sound too sweet coming from your mouth, stop it.

TASHA   No.

JAYQUESE   Oh so youse a roughneck ballerina.

TASHA   Ignorant, I'm not a ballerina. Geeze, does anyone take what I say seriously? Everyone thinks they know what's best for me.

JAYQUESE   Pops at it again? *(her father)* What's the old dog's problem?

TASHA   Huh?

JAYQUESE   I don't know why rich people don't like po people when they family's just as dysfunctional.

TASHA   My family is not dysfunctional. I'm talking about you. Why do you have to put on this show, like you know what's best for me. It's like you have to protect me because I'm some naïve little White girl.

JAYQUESE   You are a naïve little White girl.

TASHA   No I'm not, I'm not. *(pause)* I was going to give you the keys to my place; in case you wanted to get away from it all.

JAYQUESE   Your moms'll have a nice surprise.

TASHA   My mother wouldn't care. Anyway it's my place.

JAYQUESE   Remember you said you're not naïve.

TASHA   Yes.

JAYQUESE   Yuh ain't doing a good job of convincing right now.

TASHA   Jay I've told you a thousand times my folks are very liberal.

JAYQUESE   They smoked pot in the sixties and shouted freedom slogans, aight they're liberal.

TASHA   Don't mock me.

JAYQUESE   All this bullshit you're talking about mocks my 22 years of living.

TASHA   How could I seriously come from such an environment?

JAYQUESE   You'd be surprised how many White girls suck Black dicks cause White dicks remind them of their fucked up fathers.

TASHA   So you've become an expert on why White women perform fellatio.

JAYQUESE   Hey I specified Black cock, not White cock. It's political baby. Sex is political.

TASHA   So I'm your political statement?

JAYQUESE   Yeh.

TASHA   Get out of my house!

JAYQUESE   Apartment.

TASHA   GET OUT OF MY APARTMENT!!

JAYQUESE   Don't you want to know the statement?

TASHA   No.

JAYQUESE   *(holds her)* My statement is that sex with you is as good as sex with a sister…. It just be that there's a lot of White girls who suck dick, of the Black persuasion, whose daddys ain't too hallal on it.

TASHA   I'm sure that Black fathers don't like the idea of their daughters performing fellatio on Black men either.

JAYQUESE   Stop saying fellatio it sounds like a disease. Tash, if a father can't deal with the fact that his twenty-year-old daughter is sucking dick, it's triple by-pass time when he finds out it's Black.

TASHA   So it's political when… you say hello to my little friend? Because you know you work it like a man who has been abstaining for twenty-two years.

JAYQUESE   Naahh… that's something completely different. White pussy is the breeding ground of the White world. Like when you're up in there, your tongue hitting against dem lips, it's like you spanking away the demons and the more vigorous you move the tongue the more demons ass you kick. And when baby moans, climaxing, it's like a purification. Then you keep lacin with that tongue leaving your mark. *(smiles)*

TASHA   Is that what's running through your mind when I am thinking that you're trying to please me?

JAYQUESE   No Tash. Women like that shit; so niggas be doing it pretending they don't. Fact is if they wasn't there would be an epidemic of Black lesbians roaming these streets.

TASHA   But you sounded so convinced.

JAYQUESE   B, believe me niggas today ain't got time for politics, they only have time for pussy.

TASHA   If you're only here for puhssy *(mocks him)* or politics, I don't want you. Anyway I don't think like that when I'm with you.

JAYQUESE   Sure? Don't be ashamed that you were drawn to me cause I'm Black.

TASHA   Even if that had something to do with it, it's not about that anymore.

JAYQUESE   Hey, we go in wanting one thing, come out wanting something else. Ain't nothing wrong with that, intentions always change.

TASHA   Like right now.

JAYQUESE   What?

TASHA   I want to say something but I want to do something that's completely different.

JAYQUESE   Which one would I like better?

TASHA   The doing part.

JAYQUESE   I know that's the part you'd like better. *(pause)*

TASHA   I prayed to God last night.

JAYQUESE   You praying to the wrong nigga.

TASHA   I asked him not to change anything about our relationship.

JAYQUESE   Tash baby, that's me and you, we effect that he don't.

TASHA   I see something beautiful and I want to have it.

JAYQUESE   Lemme braid your hair.

TASHA   You want to braid my hair?

JAYQUESE   Don't it relax you?

TASHA   Yes, it does.

JAYQUESE   Come on then, move that sweet ass and make room.

TASHA   Okay?

JAYQUESE   Hell no, you're squashing my balls…. That's better.

TASHA   What were you thinking when you first saw me, standing at the bus stop?

JAYQUESE   She ain't sucking on a lollipop.

TASHA   Come on.

JAYQUESE   You want the ghetto real.

TASHA   Yes I want the ghetto real.

JAYQUESE   But you ain't ghetto!

TASHA   Come on Jay.

JAYQUESE   I was thinking… if I get you in bed I better not disappoint.

TASHA   The very first time?

JAYQUESE   Fuh sure.

TASHA   Jay, do you like where you are in the world?

JAYQUESE   What question is that.

TASHA   This lifestyle. *(pause)*

JAYQUESE   You knew how you met me. *(pause)*

TASHA   I know. But you just told me that intentions always change.

JAYQUESE   Okay, no playing, Tasha, speak your mind.

TASHA   I'm in love with you, I really am, I really am… well?

JAYQUESE   What?

TASHA   I want to be more than this late night rendez-vous. I want to be the most selfish woman in the world and have you all to myself. Have you in the middle of the day, have you first thing in the morning. I want us to have sex without a condom regularly, because we trust each other; not as a once-a-week risk because we didn't have any. I'm not a hoe, you know that. I don't want to ever feel insecure and think of myself as a hoe.

> *JAYQUESE puts his hands over her mouth and kisses her passionately. Lights go to black.*

SCENE FOUR

Lights come up on the boys. TUPAC has started a rap.

TUPAC   She tried to convince me,
She's more than some tits and a thong
I'm like ma
What's wrong with some tits and a thong
She said she got brains and a dream
We ain't so different

Many nights when I'm hard
I'm getting brains in my dream
Nappy head girl had enuff of the streets
Nuff of legs spread, just getting them beat
Nuff of ho'in
For some crack or something to eat
Nuff of niggas
Just fondling her dreams
Now she swear that she seeing it all slip away
And tomorrow/ain't gonna be no different than today
She switchin it up/tryna blame me for her life
But once she started ho'in/she could never be my wife
My dick musta reminded her of a dick she once knew
The one that mistook her dreams for her pussy when he started to screw
Ouuuuuee
Maybe the penetration was nice
But it shouldn'ta been enough/to make her trade in her life
Ouuuuuee
Maybe the strokin was stiff
But each time he pound the meat/it was like reloading the clip
Click!! Click!! *(motions gun)*

JEROME   Got damn.

TRINI   You ain't finish it.

TUPAC   That's how it ends.

TRINI   Naw, do the end over for meh.

TUPAC   My dick musta reminded her of a dick she once knew
The one that mistook her dreams for her pussy when he started to screw
Ouuue
Maybe the penetration was nice
But it shouldn'ta been enough/to make her trade in her life
Ouuue
Maybe the strokin was stiff
But each time he pound the meat/it was like reloading the clip...

TRINI   Now she crying in meh arms
Like I should do something right
But you know I'm just trying to get some pussy tonight.
Get some pussy tonight!

JEROME   *(laughs)* You need help.

> *LEXUS enters from the other end of the stage.*

TUPAC   I second that emotion.

TRINI   PUHHHSSY TONIGHT!

LEXUS   Jerome! Jerome!

JEROME   Damn. Lemme see what the noise is about.

JEROME walks over to LEXUS.

What you doing bawling out my name?

LEXUS   I was just calling you over.

JEROME   You know better than to be bawling out my name like that.

LEXUS   Well shit, you want me to go somewhere else?

JEROME   You know your ass ain't got no money, you can go where the fuck you want.

LEXUS   I ain't got no money?

JEROME   You ain't got no money, and you're not putting your mouth on my dick no more.

LEXUS   Who said I wanna put my mouth on that mouth floss dick of yours.

JEROME   *(smiles)* You know if it wasn't you, that would be a case for a pimp slap right there.

LEXUS   You can't hit Lex.

JEROME   You came just to give me grief ma?

LEXUS   Hmmmm… no. *(smiles)*

JEROME   How come you so playful tonight?

LEXUS   I dunno, I just had my spirits lifted.

JEROME   Spirits lifted?

LEXUS   Yeh, I just seen an old friend.

JEROME   Who that?

LEXUS   Don't worry about it.

JEROME   You talking shit to me?

LEXUS   I'm serious.

JEROME   Heart attack?

LEXUS   Heart attack!

JEROME   So you gonna tell me who the nigga is or what?

LEXUS   I told you don't worry about it.

JEROME   Hey, it don't matter either way.

LEXUS   Good to hear that, Jerome, cause I still ain't telling.

JEROME   You ain't gonna hold a man with an attitude like that.

LEXUS   Hold a man? *(laughs)* Oh shit Jerome! Who the fuck tryna hold a man? Ya'll some malicious motherfuckers.

JEROME   Ohh, you putting me on the same boat?

LEXUS   You got balls?

JEROME   Yeh.

LEXUS   You in that Titanic. Don't get me wrong, some of ya'll assholes are worse than others.

JEROME   And where does that old friend of yours stand?

LEXUS   Don't worry about it Jerome. *(smiles)*

JEROME   Aight, you on your game tonight. Can't slip shit past you. What you want from me?

LEXUS   I want a pebble.

JEROME   Lexus there's no free loading. If you can't up with the money I can't up with the shit.

LEXUS   I got money.

JEROME   Stop bullshitting, we been there, we done that.

>   *LEXUS holds out the cash.*

JEROME   Who the hell you rob?

LEXUS   This is clean money.

JEROME   I don't care if it clean or dirty. With all that money you only want a pebble?

LEXUS   This is my last hit Jerome. I'm gonna buy me some clothes, I'm just gonna clean up.

JEROME   Yeh?

LEXUS   I got a baby and shit Jerome. I gotta take care of things.

JEROME   Aight.

>   *Lights go to black.*

BEATDOWN #3

Camera angle back to the sleeping child. The bedsheets are getting wet as he pees himself. Startled, he awakens in darkness—all you see is an outline and the whites of his eyes.

SCENE FIVE

Cut back to TASHA's room, they are still kissing passionately.

TASHA   Who invented that kiss?

JAYQUESE   We did.

TASHA   It's just ours?

JAYQUESE   Baby I'ma never "honey dip" with anybody else.

TASHA   That makes me feel good.

JAYQUESE   And this? *(bites her neck)*

TASHA   That makes me feel good too.

JAYQUESE   Then I'll do it again…

TASHA   Jay. *(holds his face, then puts his hand on her belly)*

JAYQUESE   You should be rubbing my belly. I ain't rubbing your belly.

TASHA   Put your hands back.

JAYQUESE   If I put my hands back I'm gonna get devious thoughts.

TASHA   Jay.

JAYQUESE   Okay, how you like?

TASHA   Jayquese you know you'd be a great father.

JAYQUESE   Maybe, maybe not, but I don't need to think about that.

TASHA   There's no doubt in my mind you would.

JAYQUESE   If you say so. *(kisses her belly)*

TASHA   Jayquese, I'm pregnant. *(pause)*

JAYQUESE   What?

> *TASHA laughs.*

Think you'se a comedian. *(laughs)*

TASHA   I'm pregnant.

JAYQUESE   Are you serious, or are you still jerking me off?

TASHA   I'm serious.

JAYQUESE   Why the fuck are you laughing?

TASHA   I don't know.

JAYQUESE   Well listen to me, that's the past tense, you were pregnant. Cause you're not having that baby.

TASHA   You want me to have an abortion?

JAYQUESE   I'm not having a kid.

TASHA   I'm the one having it.

JAYQUESE   I don't care whose hole it drops out of, I'm not having no kid.

TASHA   You want me to have an abortion?

JAYQUESE   YES!

TASHA   Jay, let's sit down and talk about it.

JAYQUESE   Talking didn't get this kid and talking ain't gonna get rid of it so fuck talking.

TASHA   I didn't think you'd be this angry.

JAYQUESE   You didn't think what?

TASHA   This angry.

JAYQUESE   This angry?

TASHA   No!

JAYQUESE   Oh no, you were expecting old Jay to hug you and say thank you for this half-breed bastard.

TASHA   How can you say that.

JAYQUESE   With the same ease you ruined my day.

TASHA   It wasn't easy for me to tell you.

JAYQUESE   Well doesn't that just change everything.

TASHA   I didn't expect it… but I wasn't angry when I found out.

JAYQUESE   Why would you be angry? All that time telling me you were on the pill, when you'se just waiting for that half-breed.

TASHA   No.

JAYQUESE   What, you wanted curly hair?

TASHA   I was on the pill.

JAYQUESE   Was? But then you stopped?

TASHA   I never stopped. How can you think I'd be that petty. Go through hell for curly hair?

JAYQUESE   You never stopped. So what you saying, I got super sperm?

TASHA   Don't do this to me, Jay.

JAYQUESE   If you wanted a Black man, there are a lot of better candidates to have a kid with.

TASHA   You approached me don't forget that.

JAYQUESE   Hugging me up, when you knew, you knew,

TASHA   Jay!

JAYQUESE   Devious. So devious.

TASHA   Jay it's not that bad.

JAYQUESE   No you're wrong there, it's fucking bad. I mean real fucking bad. You think you can handle having a little kid?

TASHA   We can handle.

JAYQUESE   We can't handle shit. I'ma drug dealer okay, ain't no more to it.

TASHA   You're much more.

JAYQUESE   You're fucking smart, do I look like somebody's father? Do I look like I can, I can be somebody's father? You're a smart girl you're not stupid.

TASHA   Maybe you are.

JAYQUESE   Baby you're right, I'm stupid enough to know that I ain't having no baby.

TASHA   We can work through it.

JAYQUESE   Oh we can work through it alright, me, you, your mom, your dad.... If you understood this world, if you knew how nasty it was, you'd thank me for good advice. This ain't no world for no kid.

TASHA   You're an expert about everything, you know how everything works.

JAYQUESE   I don't know anything.

TASHA   You know. You know so much and still you can't be man enough to just admit that it's me. Me and my intimidating White face.

JAYQUESE   Yes it's you and your intimidating White face, good enough to screw but not good enough to have a baby with.

TASHA   I can handle that.

JAYQUESE   (yells) Ahhh! It has nothing to do with that. I'm through with politricks. You've known from the start niggas don't have time for that shit no more.

TASHA   You're through with me.

JAYQUESE   I'm not saying I'm through with you. I'm saying I'm not having no kid.

TASHA   Then you're through with me.

JAYQUESE   Don't say shit you can't live by.

TASHA   Get out.

JAYQUESE   Tasha…

TASHA   Get out!

JAYQUESE   You know what, fuck it, if that's how you wanna make your bed, make your bed.

TASHA   (sobs) You disappoint me. (pause)

JAYQUESE   I disappoint you? I disappoint you…. What can I say baby, I'm an asshole, no doubt. But I ain't nobody's father.

> Lights fade to black.

SCENE SIX

> Lights come up on a street corner where the boys are shooting the shit…

TRINI   No lie guy, lemme finish.

TUPAC   Go on, Son.

TRINI   So I'm watching this Filipino ting.

TUPAC   Takin after you, Jerome.

JEROME   Whatever.

TRINI   So I give she my neutron bomb lyrics…

TUPAC   Hun steps back…

TRINI   Steps back and points to she crotch.

JEROME   Yo nigga yo!

TRINI   Check this, she say she kitty cat was meant to roam, an no man's puttin no leash on it.

TUPAC   Son Trini was like comatose.

JEROME   So what you do Trin?

TRINI   The Red, White, Black must represent!

TUPAC   No doubt!

JEROME   For sure!

TRINI   Makin the long short. I get she home and I hittin she from the back doggy style…

TUPAC   Get at me dog…

TRINI   …Meh fingers grabbin on she ass. And ah makin all kinds ah fucked up faces you know. So I'm strokin she long dick banana boat style, Huh, Huh! Huh! She starts bawling, "I only want you, I only want you, ah nigga, ah nigga."

JEROME   Thunder Trini, thunder!

TRINI   So I jump off she ass like meh motorbike bout to crash. Bang! Grab she head with meh hand, ram she face right up in front of meh dick and ask she if she want this. She say, "Yes Daddy."

TUPAC   Do the accent.

TRINI   "Yes Daddy, give it to me hard."

JEROME   So.

TRINI   So I grab meh dick with one hand, no I lie I grab meh dick with two hands. I tell she, "this dog, meh dick, like to chase kitty cat and no run ah de mill puss is gonna put a leash on me."

TUPAC   AHH! Nigga no! Nigga!

TRINI   And I up and gone like a hungry refugee.

TUPAC   Bitches need that now and then. Hoes get all caught up on the fact they got a pussy, thinking they's royalty.

TRINI   Even the ones with stink platypus pussy.

JEROME   What the hell is a platypus pussy?

TRINI   Long lips like a duck. When you blow on it, it does blow back in your face like a fan.

TUPAC   That is slack.

TRINI   But it good in the summer when it's hot though. Nothing like some good pussy air conditioning.

TUPAC   P-A-C, pussy air con.

JEROME   Pussy air con, filthy!

TUPAC I'm sayin this though, if a bitch is gonna be slack up in a joint she must expect a nigga to be slack up on her joint.

JEROME Yeh, yeh. Just watch the shit you learning from Trini.

TUPAC It's real though, screw this double standard shit. I'ma fuck a slack bitch, I'm a slack nigga when I wanna.

TRINI Ah hole is a hole is a hole. All pussy looks red and taste like catfish. No politics to it.

JEROME Wrong, wrong. Pussy, every pussy has an individual flavour.

TUPAC Na, na, na, na.

JEROME You niggas is raw. You ain't taking the time to understand your hole. That's why you be sharing with 5, 6, niggas, cause you don't know when your holes been contaminated. You don't want to be tasting no man's Heineken.

TRINI My lips ain't tastin no pussy.

TUPAC My lips ain't tastin no pussy!

JEROME Well I'ma taste pussy for all you dogs.

TRINI Yeh right, I'll taste my own.

JEROME I knew you been hittin it.

TRINI I been leavin that shit sore!!

JEROME And I know Pac been hittin it.

TUPAC I don't eat nothing raw. I look Japanese mutherfucker! *(phone goes off)* Ah fuck that torpedo tit bitch is blowin up my shit.

TRINI You need to tell yuh girl that you runnin ah business.

TUPAC I had to put the shit on vibrator now it got my dick all hard.

JEROME No need to share that shit with us.

TRINI You need to slap that bitch up, and file she nipple down before it poke yuh eye out. Jerome, look at that nigga's neck. See all them dark mark... she nipple.

JEROME Ha! ha!

TUPAC Trini that's watless. It's a hickey dog.

JEROME Nigga whaaat! What you doing with a hickey, you too old for that. You can't be hanging with the men, and doing that boyish shit.

TUPAC She's a freak man.

TRINI She's a soukouyah.

TUPAC She's tight!!

JEROME   Nigga you fuckin sixteen-year-olds?

TUPAC   She ain't sixteen, she ain't sixteen, she be like eighteen.

JEROME   You have an eighteen-year-old blowin up your spot like this. Nigga this is a business. How many times do I have to put that in your head. Tell that bitch to ease up. You ain't give her that next number?

TUPAC   Yo, I'm schooled to this game. She ain't got that.

JEROME   You can't have no woman messing with this business.

TRINI   Ain't no trusting any ah dem bitches. They faulty. You fuck one of dem bitches, you drunk she drunk you think everything is cool. Fuck up and tell the bitch that you don't want to see she na. Next thing yuh know she starts hollerin rape. Trust meh I know that shit.

TUPAC   Jerome she's just an eighteen-year-old hole man.

JEROME   But Tupac, you like that falling in love with bitches shit.

TUPAC   Bitches fall in love with me! *(walks off)*

TRINI   Ahhh!

JEROME   So where you going?

TUPAC   Ahh… just gonna link up with Goofy.

JEROME   You must really take my Blackness for stupidity. Go on, go talk your lovey dovey in the corner.

TUPAC   Whateva, I told you, bitches fall in love with me.

> *Lights fade.*

BEAT DOWN #4

POV of the child as he gets out of bed. Camera angle—walking down the hallway. Close up of his feet walking. He reaches a bedroom door. His hands go to the doorknob to open it.

SCENE SEVEN

Light comes up on CINDY's room. The room is a little more worn out than the others. Not much in terms of a homely feeling.

CINDY   I'm glad you came. I was startin to think that you wasn't gonna be coming back, you know… I didn't mean to make you mad last time. Look I got some beer, if you want we can sit down and drink first.

JAYQUESE   I don't want to drink. Yo, why's that nigga smoking blunts round the youth?

CINDY   Well he's kinda fucked up. But it's his place too so I can't really say shit.

JAYQUESE   I thought by now your sister would have been done with that nigga.

CINDY   It's kinda hard for her.

JAYQUESE   Fuck, he broke her hand. Free-basing nigga. Shit I hate being up in this place, I should've just laid down the money and get a fucking room.

CINDY   I'm gonna find my own place.

JAYQUESE   Fuck that has to do with that?

CINDY   Then you don't have to worry about them.

JAYQUESE   Whatever, take your fucking clothes off.

CINDY   What's wrong?

JAYQUESE   What do you mean what's wrong. Take your fucking clothes off, what you think I came here to converse?

CINDY   No.

JAYQUESE   Exactly, so let's not fool ourselves, it's a booty call.

CINDY   Well I got you beer.

JAYQUESE   I can't fuck if I'm drunk. Just take your fucking clothes off. Next you'll tell me you cooked and shit.

CINDY   I didn't cook anything.

JAYQUESE   Good.

CINDY   Do you want me to rub your back?

JAYQUESE   If what I wanted was foreplay I would've just jerked off.

CINDY   So you think you can just come up in here and fuck me and not say a word?

JAYQUESE   Yeh, what do I have to say to you?

CINDY   I dunno, but just don't make it so dirty.

JAYQUESE   Who do you think you're fooling? You're a hoe, I just came here for sex. I just need to fuck some things outta my mind.

CINDY   How are you gonna call me a hoe to my face?

JAYQUESE   What! You don't think I know you fucked Tupac?

CINDY   I only dealt with Tupac because I wanted to get with you.

JAYQUESE   So you think I would think of you as a respectful girl knowing that you sharing that "nannie" with all my boys?

CINDY   After the first time we had sex, I never had it with Tupac.

JAYQUESE   That's a bullshit lie, that nigga told me.

CINDY   Maybe once, but he made it seem like I owed him.

JAYQUESE   I don't care you know. I called you, I thought you knew what this was all about.

CINDY   I swear I did it for you. I swear, swear to God I ain't been with Tupac.

JAYQUESE   Bitch stop swearing to him. That nigga got you straddling every nigga's dick.

CINDY   I'm not a hoe.

JAYQUESE   Cindy, I spent 5 bucks on these condoms, you want me to throw them away or what?

CINDY   No, but I'm not a hoe.

JAYQUESE   You being a hoe is trivial, I got a dick you got a hole, you wanna make a connection?

CINDY   Yes.

JAYQUESE   Well finish taking the clothes off. *(pause)*

CINDY   If you think that I'm dirty then why do you want to have sex with me?

JAYQUESE   I don't think you're dirty, Cindy, I don't think you're dirty.

CINDY   I know I do things, and I know it's, like it's true, right, I fucked a lot of guys but it's not like every time I wanted to.

JAYQUESE   Okay.

CINDY   No it's not okay. Cause you think I'ma hoe. You're not a woman, you can punch people, you can run faster, hide better. I wanna run, I can't. I got one weapon, and if I keep it closed long enough it's not effective, and if I keep it open too long I'm dirty. You know I feel so stupid. I feel so stupid because you making me feel the way they make me feel, and I thought you'se my angel.

JAYQUESE   I'm not an angel. Why you women putting all this on me. I'm not an angel, I'm none of that. Whatever I'm giving off it's just lying. I'm not an ANGEL.

> Loud yelling, baby crying in the next room. Pause.

Cindy, I ain't here to fool you, make you think there's anything that's going on.

CINDY   Yeh.

JAYQUESE   I just need a favour. I just need you to help me out.

CINDY   What do you need?

JAYQUESE   I came here for sex, just plain sex. I need to sweat a little, get my mind clean.

CINDY   You just need me to be a hoe. That's how I became a hoe right? By giving everybody what they need.

JAYQUESE   Baby girl, it won't make no sense to you, but I just need to sweat a little. *(pause)* This is the last time. Cindy, I won't make you a hoe no more.

They engage in the act.

Lights go to black.

BEATDOWN #5

The bedroom door is opened. The scared child sees his mother/a figure in bed. A hold on his look. He steps into the room. As his feet touch down, he plunges down the same empty hole, his hands extend upwards towards the woman.

SCENE EIGHT

Lights come up on TERINA's bedroom, JAYQUESE in his boxers TERINA in her bra and panties.

JAYQUESE   I can't deal with this day to day anymore.

TERINA   What do you mean?

JAYQUESE   I don't walk like a black panther no more. I walk like a pussy.

TERINA   You been hard your whole life.

JAYQUESE   I walk all uncertain and full of fear.

TERINA   At times we all do.

JAYQUESE   I think about death on the regular. It's like the man's telling me it's my turn.

TERINA   You got a full life.

JAYQUESE   Death… I walk the streets like a pussy, thinking about dying. About not knowing who'll be at my side or if someone's going to remember me one year later.

TERINA   You know we all have short memories.

JAYQUESE   I know. But my frustration's just getting me off. When I'm thinking about death it be like I wanna puke. The shit is in my stomach and it's in my throat, and it's thick, my balls get hard. My dick just shrivels up. I can't... B am I alone in this? Are my niggas going through this?

TERINA   We're all gonna die. At some point they're gonna think about it.

JAYQUESE   It scares the shit outta me.

TERINA   It scares me too.

JAYQUESE   Yeh?

TERINA   Fuck yeh. Cause it's just this big uncertainty.

JAYQUESE   B, there be nights when I'm walking alone. Nobody on the streets. And I look at the asphalt and it don't make sense. I look at the stars and they make sense, I can't say what the sense is, but they make it. I wanna touch them.

TERINA   You wanna do that?

JAYQUESE   Yeh I wanna sit on one.

TERINA   You'll burn.

JAYQUESE   So what if I burn.

TERINA   You burn you're gone. I won't have... no one will have you.

JAYQUESE   I'm like an alien on this shit earth baby, I don't belong here.

TERINA   Now you sound like a pussy. I mean being scared is natural, but not wanting to fight to survive, that's, that's weak. You gotta be a man about it all. You gotta be a man.

JAYQUESE   You want me to be a man about it all huh? What's manhood?

TERINA   Strength, pride, laying claim to what is yours and fighting for it.

JAYQUESE   You born with it? You gotta gain it? Can you lose it?

TERINA   Well you're born a man so I guess you're born with it.

JAYQUESE   When did it come about, was it the first time I got fucked? Was it the first time I jumped a punk?

TERINA   That shit ain't got nothing to do with manhood.

JAYQUESE   If a man steps to you in a jam, you want your boy to fight for you right?

TERINA   Well not fight but...

JAYQUESE   That's manhood right? Like a lion, takin care of his.

TERINA   That lion thing is something different.

JAYQUESE   I give it to you good right? Touch you how you like?

TERINA   Yes.

JAYQUESE   But that ain't manhood though. Cause I still feel pussy this very moment.

TERINA   Wake up. Why do you need to define it, Jay? What the hell does that have to do with treating your woman right, doing right by your seeds. Maybe it's nothing more than some bullshit that we use to antagonize.

JAYQUESE   You don't get it. You look at me with those female eyes and you can't feel my feel.

TERINA   I never professed that I can feel all you feel. I just don't want you getting messed up over this. Men spend their entire lives debating this.

JAYQUESE   But they didn't have the urgency. They didn't feel like they lost it.

TERINA   Why do you feel like you lost it?

JAYQUESE   Cause on one hand I fear death, and just as strong as that fear is, I'm sometimes wanting to just embrace the dog. Cause I don't want to fight anymore, cause I don't understand what it is I'm fighting for. Why the hell a man would fight just to be able to fight.

TERINA   What are you fighting?

JAYQUESE   It's like I'm fighting for a bunch of faceless, nameless ghosts that are thumping at my back. Telling me the world is sinister, telling me it's unjust. They bellowing in my gut telling me I need to be angry. Like I ain't got shit to be angry about already.

TERINA   What is it they want you to fight for?

JAYQUESE   Bitch I dunno!!… sorry.

TERINA   Don't use that shit on me.

JAYQUESE   Sorry. *(pause)*

TERINA   I hear them too.

JAYQUESE   What do they say to you?

TERINA   It's just this burden to be of importance. It's like my achievement is a sort of trophy for them. Sometimes it drives me crazy; cause I work my ass off, do the education thing yet…

JAYQUESE   Break it down for me.

TERINA   My success is based on some convention that I didn't put in place. I fight myself because I question why this financial stability is success. Why my accomplishment has to be reflective of a mass of people who don't give a fuck, fuck all about what my middle class ass does. Cause no matter how Black and how proud and how righteous I am, some African is gonna tell me I'm not African. I'm not from the motherland. And some Black is gonna tell me I'm nothing but a bougie, when I'm fighting the same struggle the same fight.

JAYQUESE   They messing with you too.

TERINA   Why do I need to speak for these people. Why do I think I need to?

JAYQUESE   Terina you're bright. I can see what they want with you, hell you making moves, you going places. What they want with me, a corner boy?

TERINA   Maybe you are a God sent. Maybe you're meant to touch people that no one else can.

JAYQUESE   For one, I don't believe in no God. No Allah, no Tyrone, no saviour that don't save nobody.

TERINA   My faith isn't strong enough to sell you on it Jay. But maybe you're going nuts and filled with all these fears because the streets don't want you anymore.

JAYQUESE   They want me, they needs my soul parading up and down. They need my energy beating away at their backs, they need that most definite.

TERINA   They're haunting your ass for a reason.

JAYQUESE   The streets love me. I'm its child. That's why you're up on my Black ass. That's why I'm anything that I am.

TERINA   No. *(goes to him)* I see something beautiful in you.

JAYQUESE   That's wack.

TERINA   You're fearless *(pause)* and strong.

JAYQUESE   Not now.

TERINA   Even now. *(pause)* Your mind fascinates me. You fascinate me. It's as if you're one of those voices… I don't want you falling down the hole.

JAYQUESE   There are BeatDowns.

TERINA   Don't beat yourself down the hole. *(pause)*

JAYQUESE   You wanna hear something funny? This shit been bugging me for like days.

TERINA   Something funny?

JAYQUESE   I cried when Biggie died. *(rap singer and entertainer Notorious B.I.G.)* I poured tears for that nigga. He was young. He was making money. Got out of the hustle, had kids to take care of. And they snuff him out. I cried, because there wasn't nothing fair about it. Shit we ain't need the stress of living cause thinking about death is stressful enough. I cussed that night. Like the devil was all up in me. I swore that God didn't exist. That night, that was the night that I swore that God was an evil bastard. I said it doesn't pay to believe. Cause Biggie was beat down by some ignorant nigga. So who the fuck cares if I beat down some ignorant nigga? God don't care. The world don't really care. And I cried like a bitch. Bawling out, "why Father, why Father." Just like I'd seen my Baptist mother bawl. Then I rolled me some trees to smoke away the pain. I was in pain for this genius that no one saw as a genius. This man that worked hard. You know, did things to get by.

TERINA   Jayquese.

JAYQUESE   March 9th. In a year people ain't even gonna remember that. And I thought to myself, I won't even remember it.

TERINA   Come back to bed, your mind is just jumping.

JAYQUESE   You know what's funny. I cried like a bitch when I heard bout B.I.G. My God-fearing mother died... I didn't cry... and here I was crying like a bitch.

TERINA   Cause you loved your moms.

JAYQUESE   FUCK!... HEY I LOVE Biggie too. *(emotions start to bubble)*

TERINA   She knew Jay, she knew you loved her.

JAYQUESE   My mother was beat down, how a woman suppose to die so young.

TERINA   I can't answer that. I won't bullshit you either.

JAYQUESE   I wish you could. Terina I wish you could baby... there be days I can't say for sure I remember her voice.

TERINA   Why won't you cry now?

JAYQUESE   Manhood.

TERINA   I think now is the wrong time for that word. You need to cry.

JAYQUESE   In your Black hands?

TERINA   In my Black hands.

JAYQUESE   Loving someone is shit. Words are too complicated, they hide how you feel. We should just grunt and groan, you know that. Just the sounds of pain and ecstasy.

TERINA   Just the sounds of the soul.

JAYQUESE   Pain and ecstasy, those types of grunts and groans. Cause nobody had a right to take Biggie. He only wanted to take care of his baby girl.

TERINA   He only wanted to take care of his baby girl.

JAYQUESE   I can't make sense of it at all.

TERINA holds him.

It's all falling apart around me… Tasha just shook my world.

TERINA   What happened?

JAYQUESE   She shook it all up.

TERINA   What did she do? Talk to me Jay, you know you can talk to me.

Lights go to black.

SCENE NINE

Lights come up on TRINI in the middle of the street.

TRINI   Murder is a real weird ting. To some people it's the ultimate sin, can drive a man mad with guilt. To some the shit just the same as breathing, or passing wind *(farting)*. That's why you can't take these niggas lightly, not out here. Walcott Davids, chop meh father hand off, and jook him in the belly. I was six years old in the backseat ah Daddy's maxi. I see it all happen. Meh father ain't know what hit him, the cutlass just come down whoom!! Blood everywhere. Meh father was an ass! Stupid! He gone out there running he mouth big, and he leave he blade in the car. I mean of course the man go chop yuh, you have to have yuh ting ready. Asshole. Walcott Davids teach me a lesson, chop or get chopped. All this conscience thing they does talk about, bullshit. Conscience go get you kill. You have to be in the frame of mind where you could cut a motherfuckers leg off for nothing. I could sneak up on a nigga from the back, blow his head off. Then lick shot ten more times if the shit gets on meh shirt. It don't move me, shake me, it just a little something I must do. I eat, fuck you up, I shit. And I really don't feel, you don't have time to feel. I mean me personally I'd rather just make my niggas laugh and screw some hoes, fuh real. But get me on the wrong side and I'll put a blade to yuh neck and make you suck your own dick. Then show you how nonchalant murder is.

Lights go to black.

BEATDOWN #6

Still falling—camera angle on the child's flailing legs, then on his extended arms desperately trying to hold on to something to stop the fall. Frantic.

SCENE TEN

Lights come up on TERINA's room. This is a continuation of their previous conversation. JAYQUESE is sweating.

TERINA   This game that you're trapped in, that you're part of…. You need to sit down, I don't care if you have to get drunk or smoke up, but you need to go in recluse and think about this game. This is hell that you're inhabiting. All these niggas walking around heartless. Cause they born in this game with low self-esteem, no esteem, no self. The game just grab them up and fill them with something and they think it's esteem, but it ain't. They don't know. They can't see the overall picture it's too immense… I mean all these niggas walking around with this pumped up bravado, they ain't thinking about livin they thinking about killing. Living is just the by-product of killing first. That doesn't make any sense. You are part of this no income, no job, nowhere to go game.

JAYQUESE   I make money.

TERINA   You make money, but how do you make money? By dealing drugs. And if the White man is the devil then fuck it, Black niggas are his henchmen. Cause the devil is what's wrong and you're doing wrong. Are you the hand of the devil, Jayquese, or are you caught in the game?

JAYQUESE   The devil ain't just no White man, baby. He's too fucking smart to keep just being the White man when we done found him out. He's changing colours. He's the whole fucking world.

TERINA   Yes he is. But we killing ourselves, we making it hard to fight against what we really need to fight against. You don't feel the danger of what you're part of because your mentality is built around this danger. I know you're trying to make money, but you'll go to any extent, then the other man will go to any extent. Then we have a society of people with money who don't see life. Don't experience life because they are looking over their backs, fingers itching to fire.

JAYQUESE   Life girl, this is life. This is Darwinism, survival of the fittest, this is life. This is fighting back, this is gaining things for yourself. I'ma nigga with money in this game, I'ma nigga with a gun, that's the deadliest nigga.

TERINA   You need to quit the bullshitting Jay, you're talking to me. Money is a house, money is a car, you're small time. You busy beating your feet on the pavement. You putting your life on the line for nothing. And you alone know 50 niggas with a gun, so who's the deadliest nigga? Not to mention 100 White guys and Asians and Indians who all feel that they are the deadliest niggas.

JAYQUESE   You don't understand the game. The game's been played throughout history.

TERINA   Throughout history the only people who die are those in the game. You're all killing for the same recycled 50 dollars.

JAYQUESE   Ain't nobody dying for no 50 dollars.

TERINA   Sorry, they die for less.

JAYQUESE   I didn't write no rules.

TERINA   Why are you playing by them? If I can't understand this damn world, if I can't make sense of life and death and relationships, how are you suppose to make sense of it?

JAYQUESE   I don't make sense of it. It's not a factor in my life. I can't afford the luxury to think about that stuff.

TERINA   I know you think about it. You tremble in my arms thinking about it. *(pause)*

JAYQUESE   I came to you cause I'm stressed out. I mean that motherfucking White girl just told me she's pregnant. And now you're telling me this bullshit.

TERINA   I'm just showing you the world this kid is going to be a part of if you're not going to be in his life. Cause if your mind is made up I agree with you, let her have an abortion. And if she doesn't, grab that baby and choke the last breath out of his body. Kill him fast, don't make it as crucial as your death. We got enough little Black boys who have moms who ain't nobody's wife.

JAYQUESE   What?

TERINA   Look at you, this is a sign. That man up there or whatever, maybe this is a sign.

JAYQUESE   That motherfucker took my mother.

TERINA   And you didn't have a father to fall back on.

JAYQUESE   That motherfucker took my father.

TERINA   He told your father to leave? *(pause)*

JAYQUESE   I told that girl, "go on the pill." I even said it slowly, "go on the pill." If I knew Spanish I would've said it in Spanish too.

TERINA   You don't know if she wasn't.

JAYQUESE   It doesn't matter, what matters is that she does what needs to be done.

TERINA   Does she want the kid?

JAYQUESE   She's yelling some, "let's talk about it" shit. Like I wasn't talking when I told her to get rid of the fucking kid.

TERINA   Jayquese…

JAYQUESE   Do I look like a fucking father… be real with me, do I look like a fucking father?

TERINA   Obviously she cares about you.

JAYQUESE   That doesn't cut it in this world. You don't collect an additional 50 bucks because you care. *(pause)*

TERINA   I told you, you were brave. Don't make me look like an ass, Jay.

JAYQUESE   You should have just taken the sex and just let me be.

TERINA   Thank you, thanks.

JAYQUESE   I just cause tension, I just cause tension wherever I go.

TERINA   If push comes to shove you might not care if you have to kill somebody. I'm not sure you'd care if your girl died, but I never thought you'd want to witness yourself die again.

JAYQUESE   What?

TERINA   The baby is just you again. *(pause)*

JAYQUESE   Okay, she could have the baby… her parents have money, they can help her raise it.

TERINA   Is your head that thick? Don't you listen to anything that I say?

JAYQUESE   Well I don't know what you're saying to me, one minute you'se advising your boy to kill the kid, the next minute you're calling me a murder. What! Wha, wha, what?

TERINA   If you care about this girl, be a MAN. *(pause)*

JAYQUESE   I'ma just get my shit and leave.

> *Lights go to black.*

BEATDOWN #7

Continuation of the fall. POV—looking down until the camera slowly turns up. There is the outline of a figure looking down at the falling child.

SCENE ELEVEN

JEROME off on his own.

JEROME   We're in the middle of this heated argument; which on it's own isn't that bad. I mean I like me a little toss up every now and then. But you can't pull that shit outside of a club. Not outside of a club B. She's pissed cause she saw me pinch some girl's ass. And ma ain't backing down. In my head I'm saying "simmer," right. See I know I only got 20 seconds before I gotta do something. "Simmer, simmer down." I laid it out to her before; don't disrespect me in public, cause my choices are few. Yeh, I got caught out, she got a right to be mad. But not now, not here. Save it till we get home, don't give me pussy for a week, whateva, just not now. *(pause)* Ten seconds… "Simmer down." Five seconds. *(pause)* She shuts up. My fingers relax. I wanna smile cause she pushed it as far as she knew she could push it. Saved a little face. That's knowing the fucking streets, man. That's knowing the unwritten rules. You gotta pay attention to this shit. You gotta know when to act ignorant, and when to be silent and strong. You gotta know which nigga will say he'll kill you, and which nigga really would. Nothing random; off the cuff niggas end up dead or in jail. My brother was off the cuff, I got it in my blood. *(pause)* But I know the rules.

Lights go to black.

SCENE TWELVE

Outside in the street. JAYQUESE is walking down the street on his way toward the boys. At the beginning JAYQUESE should be at one extreme of the street, the boys at the other. While he is walking there is a voiceover of a conversation between TASHA and TERINA.

A phone rings…

TASHA Hello.

TERINA Hello, is this Tasha?

TASHA Yeah.

TERINA I'm… I'm a friend of Jayquese…

TASHA What kind of a friend?

TERINA Well, it doesn't matter. I just want you to hang in there.

TASHA Hang in there?

TERINA Let him find his way.

TASHA Did he mention something to you? Because he didn't look…

TERINA He didn't tell me, but just hang in there.

TASHA Why are you doing this?

TERINA Don't give up. *(pause)*

TASHA You know I'm White right?

TERINA Give him time.

TASHA Okay.

TERINA Okay.

TASHA Thanks. *(hangs up)*

    JAYQUESE approaches his boys on the street corner.

TUPAC I'm just putting it like this; the White girls that we meet up in the clubs are not legitimate White girls.

TRINI What yuh mean by that?

TUPAC   If we buck up on a White girl I'ma tell you straight up, huns got problems. Either she's on some "I been abused" shit or the bitch is ghetto.

JEROME   Jayquese nigga where you at?

JAYQUESE   Just been on the fringes for a hot second.

TUPAC   Now this is a nigga who knows how things run. Jay, ain't it real the White girls we meet is just messed up?

JAYQUESE   Yo, Trini knows better than me, he got three of them knocked up.

JEROME   Island boy don't care what they look like.

TRINI   Shut yuh mother cunt. What yuh think, I does be sticking my dick in any shrivel up prune?

TUPAC   Prunes does make you shit, dunn.

JEROME   Come on Trini, are your girls messed up?

TRINI   Naw... well just one.

JEROME   What's wrong with her?

TRINI   Emotionally she kinda screw up, yuh know. The first time ah talk to she, she's telling me that she was adopted and a whole buncha other shit. Plus she does talk some, "bumba clot this bumba clot that," like I'm some bloody Jamaican. Shit my name is "Trini."

TUPAC   This is my theory. To understand our shit, our music, our culture, you need to have our sensibility. And no fucking around it, we's ghetto. So the White girls that dig our shit, understand our shit on the real, either have nuff Black friends or they straight up po.

JEROME   That's bullshit, all kinda White girls dig our shit. Fuck my girl digs our shit.

TRINI   But your chick is Chinese.

JEROME   She ain't no Chinese, she's Korean.

TRINI   Same chopstick no different.

TUPAC   Both they fathers be kicking your ass.

TRINI   (*jumps up*) Ah yah! Meesta Wong chop off yuh dick and use it as ribs.

JEROME   You need to sit your ass down, Pac. You be humpin everything.

TUPAC   I ain't denying that son. I'm just illustrating the philosophies of the ghetto, you need to be understanding that. When I'm letting out lyrics I'm documenting that. "As it is said let it be written" word!

JEROME   You ain't got nothing to say Jay?

TUPAC Come, kid, drop some knowledge on these knuckleheads.

JAYQUESE I'ma just let ya'll argue.

JEROME You best say something before these two start wilding.

TRINI How come you didn't come up at the club?

JAYQUESE Sometimes a nigga just needs time to think.

TRINI Bouncer got stabbed up in the joint. He was pulling some "King Kong" I'ma motherfucker styles, when this wild crazy youth come and give him some King Kong in his ribs.

TUPAC Bitch was calling for his mother and shit.

JEROME Messed up business for the rest of the night.

JAYQUESE First I hear ah that.

TUPAC Real?

TRINI You been up in yuh room all weekend?

JAYQUESE Naw, just ain't had my head to the street.

JEROME If you out here you know you have to have your head to the street.

TRINI Locked in.

TUPAC No doubt.

JEROME No doubt.

JAYQUESE I feel yuh.

JEROME Ain't no room for lapsing.

TRINI Yeh.

JEROME Ain't no room, you hear me?

JAYQUESE Yeh, no doubt.

TUPAC Check this nigga, "ain't no room."

TRINI "No room! The roach motel full!"

JEROME Go on, you hard heads act like you ain't understanding.

TUPAC Why there so much tension out here? Brothers be feeling the moon and shit.

TRINI Obeah is in the air. Make sure you take a bush bath.

JAYQUESE Stop your small island talk.

TRINI Yuh saying that now, wait till they put something on yuh. Small island? We go see small island when yuh beggin God.

TUPAC   And you know niggas ain't believing that shit.

JAYQUESE   Niggas most definite don't believe that shit. And you don't believe that shit Trini.

TRINI   I don't have to believe none ah that. I fucked a Baptist back home, and she say she go use she pussy power to protect me.

JEROME   How are you gonna hit a Baptist?

TRINI   With some nice sweet sugarcane strokes.

JAYQUESE   You love to talk shit.

TUPAC   Next thing he knows, that Baptist thing got a kid for him.

TRINI   I got enough.

JAYQUESE   How many you claim?

TRINI   Three.

TUPAC   Three little half-breed pickney.

JEROME   And he don't even check them.

TRINI   I drop off Pampers when I go for a screw, so don't talk that shit.

TUPAC   Nigga, you be buying maxi pads not no Pampers.

JAYQUESE   How your boy doing?

TUPAC   He's two now.

JAYQUESE   Yeh, how's he doing?

JEROME   He don't be talking to the bitch no more.

TUPAC   Seriously, the mother's checking some other kid. I ain't got time for that.

TRINI   Yuh should never have time for that. They need to recognize who the kings are.

JAYQUESE   You said that kid was going to be Jordan.

TUPAC   He still is. His name is still Jordan.

JAYQUESE   You were up at that girls crib every day when that kid was born.

TUPAC   Yeh.

JEROME   He bought a full size basketball for that kid, bigger than the youth.

TRINI   I bought a condom for mines, mini's.

TUPAC   Me and the moms ain't seeing eye to eye. We ain't really cared for each other.

TRINI   That's what she told you!

TUPAC   It's true though. I didn't take time to see it. Whateva, lesson learned.

JEROME   Fuck it, if that nigga wanna take care of your kid let him take care of your kid.

JAYQUESE   He ain't care bout shit except pussy. You know none of us taking care of no broad's kid.

TUPAC   No doubt!

TRINI   For sure!

JEROME   No doubt!

JAYQUESE   Jordan huh? Shit… Jerome you got a surprise?

JEROME   You know Jerome always double-bagging that shit.

TRINI   Brown-baggin don't count.

JEROME   You should try that, Trini.

TRINI   I have foreskin and that the only skin that I pulling on this dick.

TUPAC   Wait till your dick falls off. How you gonna live with no dick Trini?

TRINI   Don't even joke.

JEROME   Trini can't be living with no dick.

JAYQUESE   You got the five finger, Trini.

TRINI   Trini don't play with none ah that five finger shit. Don't joke man, that's the only thing I got.

TUPAC   How come you got no seeds Jay?

TRINI   You does fuck more than anybody.

JEROME   Bitches always on that tip.

TUPAC   You probably triple-bagging it.

TRINI   He probably duct-taping he tottie.

JEROME   That's small island shit!

TUPAC   Huh, Jay? You got some on-the-down low?

JAYQUESE   Whatever, man.

JEROME   Bitches know better than to bring that shit to Jay.

JAYQUESE   I don't know, I don't got them powers anymore.

JEROME   Nigga you still powerful like the motherfucking day.

TUPAC   Just count yuh blessings. You don't have to feel guilty.

JAYQUESE   You feel guilty kid?

TUPAC   It's my youngin, right, no matter what it's my youngin. You feel me?

JAYQUESE   I feel you. *(pause)*

TRINI   I know them girls does be using that guilt shit to make me stay with them, ain't happening.

JEROME   Any woman who gets with us, knowing our situation, knowing we's scratching to get those dollars, bitches better know what they gonna get.

JAYQUESE   I'm saying!

TUPAC   I'm saying too!

TRINI   They not fucking listening though!

TUPAC   And there ain't no way nigga's gonna stop from fucking.

TRINI   Pussy is God's only gift to the Black man.

TUPAC   That's why our dicks' so fucking big.

JEROME   You buggin. Give these niggas a subject and they start buggin.

JAYQUESE   That's some bullshit consolation prize.

TUPAC   But you know we'll take it.

TRINI   No doubt!

JEROME   No doubt!

JAYQUESE   Fuck, no doubt!

JEROME   It always gonna be like this ain't it?

TUPAC   Is a nigga always gonna try to get a dime? Is people just always gonna be thinking we's lazy? Is Black people gonna be scared to claim us? Fuck, the game ain't never gonna change, just the playas.

TRINI   And the rest of the world playa hating.

TUPAC   But the world ain't ready for me though.

JEROME   Nobody ready for you.

TUPAC   They better be, cause I'ma hit them with that...
"undisputed heavyweight champion of the world Muhammad Ali shit.
Bite your ear spit it out in the ring Mike Tyson shit
Fuck my best friend's girl, then tell him that I'm sorry shit
Be on my baby mother's nipple, suckin on that milk shit
Have my little baby saying, Daddy, you gonna leave me some of that shit..."

TRINI   Nigga freestyle.

TUPAC   "...I'm bringing you the real live shit
Remedial class type shit
Size you up eye to eye forget fuck or fight
You ready to fly kinda shit
I'm talking the real dog ghetto shit.
Ain't got nothing to live for shit
Fuck your girl while you watching shit
Hit you in the stomach so hard that you shit bricks shit!"

JEROME   Nigga whaaa! Cold!

TRINI   Nice, that's all, NICE!

JAYQUESE   That ain't no freestyle, nigga rehearsed that shit till it was memorized. Trini show him some hardcore freestyle.

TUPAC   HOT BUTTA BABY!

TRINI   I gonna do the same shit, kinda song.
"Trini style, lyrically fly, step in with thunder
Take your girl from right under you eye shit..."

Continues to adlib, different freestyle each performance.

...Now I pass it to my nigga Rome."

JEROME   *(does his own freestyle)* "...Yo, Jay take a sip of this..."

JAYQUESE   *(does a freestyle)* "...Ah shit broke my own rhyme."

TUPAC   Yo, we tight with ours! This could be some G-UNIT shit!

JAYQUESE   You're the only nigga with lyrics, kid.

TUPAC   Look man, I'm gonna document this shit life we live. Get paid for living foul.

JAYQUESE   I feel you. Maybe we get a demo for your ass.

JEROME   You backing this nut?

JAYQUESE   Can't knock a nigga for dreaming.

JEROME   True.

TRINI   You guys is crazy. All that talk, all that is just crazy.

TUPAC   You gonna get your piece, Trini.

TRINI   Dreaming is one thing you can depend on to fuck up a nigga.

JAYQUESE   Is that word?

TRINI   Word!

TUPAC   Just because you don't understand this music thing, don't mean you have to shit on a nigga.

TRINI   I ain't shittin on you.

JEROME   Ain't that your bitch over there?

TUPAC   Damn, we see who is really wearing the pants. I mean pan*ties*. *(smiles)*

TRINI   I told she about this.

> *TRINI gets up and walks towards the female. Both are still visible. JEROME and JAYQUESE walk to a different section of the stage. There are three different scenes. TUPAC takes out his phone, but doesn't dial. He simply holds it as he contemplates it. All three scenes are visible.*

Somebody better be dead, cause I don't know what you doing here. Yuh can't just be showing up making my boys feel I soft.

JEROME   I don't know about these cats, they gonna mess up.

JAYQUESE   What you feeling?

JEROME   Like Pac, he's only in the game so he could write those lyrics and say that he lived the life.

JAYQUESE   I feel yuh.

JEROME   If you looking to jump out of the game, don't be in the game, cause these niggas in the game don't have time for you.

JAYQUESE   But Pac ain't trying to hear that.

JEROME   Niggas out here are done jealous, him going around saying he's Tupac.

JAYQUESE   He just loving that HiP-HoP. He knows that shit.

JEROME   If he studied the game the same way he'd be set.

JAYQUESE   I don't know, maybe it's just not his focus. But Pac's cool.

> *TUPAC dials, and starts a phone conversation with his baby momma.*

TUPAC   What's really good?—I woke you up, I never knew you to be sleeping this early.

JEROME   And Trini just getting wild. Every day it's like he's more crazy. He thinks he can get away with more shit. Nigga's sloppy with his, if he ain't careful he'll be up with my brother.

JAYQUESE   Word! You heard from that kid?

JEROME   No.

JAYQUESE   That's your blood, you got to check up on him. Make sure he keeps his head. Prison bars are cold enough, you can't be cold to your brother.

JEROME   Being up in there fills your head with negative ideas, I can't handle that.

JAYQUESE   The world is negative.

JEROME   I feel yuh.

TUPAC   Nahh, we talking now I ain't need to call back—Why you whisperin for, somebody in bed with you—Two seconds and you start throwing shit in my face. Go on tell me what kinda job he holding, throw that at me too.

JEROME   You know Moms ill yo.

JAYQUESE   Naw, for real?

JEROME   She got a brain tumour.

JAYQUESE   When you seeing her?

JEROME   I ain't seeing her.

JAYQUESE   Nigga that's your moms.

JEROME   She don't want to see me.

JAYQUESE   How you know that?

JEROME   She disowned me at sixteen.

JAYQUESE   You know you was off the chain back then. Your mother just pissed you was following your brother. Your mother cares.

JEROME   Nigga, if anybody's mother cared it was yours. Your momma worked her ass for you.

JAYQUESE   Yours did the same.

JEROME   My mother had like fifty niggas running about. Have me calling them uncle. Motherfuckers weren't my uncle. A young nigga shouldn't be seeing that.

TUPAC   I ain't call in a month because of this shit, move on I'm calling now— I called all calm and you still blow up at me cause you mad.

JAYQUESE   You needed food on your table.

JEROME   You had food on your table, your momma didn't do that shit.

JAYQUESE   So what? She ended up dead before your mother.

JEROME   Nigga you don't know what you had.

TUPAC   I know you still heated at me, and I don't know half the shit you heated at. I don't know what it is you still holding against me.

JAYQUESE   Nigga I know what I had, and I know what I lost.

JEROME   If that woman dies she'll be happier not knowing about me.

JAYQUESE   Man you can't say that, all we got is our mothers.

JEROME   WHY?

JAYQUESE   Niggas... niggas...

TUPAC   I'm not fuckin selfish. Right now I'm trying to be big about things and you all up in my ear.

JEROME   It don't matter. I don't think she needs to be reminded of her past.

JAYQUESE   Which hospital she up at?

JEROME   She ain't at no hospital, she wants to die in that apartment. Don't blame her, that's what killed her.

TUPAC   What you wanna keep pinning things on me. Be mad at me for the rest of your life—Things is bigger than just me and you.

JAYQUESE   I can't tell you how to live your life, nigga.

JEROME   I'm gonna buy her a big motherfucking tombstone though. With gold engraving.

JAYQUESE   Gold.

TUPAC   You need to grow the fuck up.

JEROME   You better know!!

TUPAC   Screw this shit! Talk to you in a year, tell Jordan I love him. *(hangs up)* Shit.

TRINI   Bitch!

> *TRINI is kicking the girl in her stomach. She starts screaming loudly.*

JAYQUESE   Fuck Trini's gonna kill her.

> *They rush over.*

TUPAC   Nigga wow!

JAYQUESE   Hold the nigga.

> *TRINI keeps kicking her.*

JEROME   *(slaps him)* Stop the shit! *(TRINI stops.)*

JAYQUESE   What the fuck you doing?

TRINI   Bitch told me she's pregnant for some other nigga. I'ma kill that seed.

TUPAC   She pregnant now?

TRINI   Fuck yeh.

JAYQUESE   You probably killed the kid.

TRINI   I hope so.

JEROME   You can't be doin that in public.

JAYQUESE   Fuck can't leave her here. Ya'll get her off the street.

TUPAC   She's unconscious.

JEROME   Is she dead?

TUPAC   No, just unconscious.

TRINI   Gonna come telling me that shit. *(He breaks loose and hits her again.)*

JAYQUESE   Stop nigga. You guys just lift her up and get her out of here. Find a clinic or something. Come on, What! What!

> *They exit with her. JAYQUESE looks around him, touches his stomach, then starts a steady walk which turns into a run. He runs until his legs can no longer support the strain. Exhausted, he stops again, looking around. Holds his stomach one more time, bending over to throw up.*
>
> *His head is mad dizzy, buzzing with a million bees. He struggles to compose himself, closing his eyes. The projection screen comes up showing the image of the person looking down the hole... completely weakened, he lifts his head to the sky.*

BEATDOWN #8

> *As he lifts his head, he sees the outline of the image. It is as if it's looking down at him. He hunches over.*

JAYQUESE   Why God? You been breaking me down all my life. Everything that meant something to me you took it away. I'm in a world with a billion people and you got me feeling so alone. You got me walking alone. Just take me, and end this shit!

> *Leaving the hunched position, he swings his head up to the sky. As he does this, the blurry figure comes into focus. It is a grown man—his father.*

(He is completely overcome with emotion. Pause.) You been watching me in this motherfucker? How long? How long you been watching me? How it seem to you from there, you think I'm liking this? Talk to me, I wanna hear your voice. My whole life I wanted to hear your voice. It didn't matter that I couldn't see you, I wanted to hear your voice. *(pause)* I use'ta think my daddy was a handsome nigga. Can't nobody put nothing on him. Can't nobody— I been looking in the mirror, my jawline coming in like yours. Just like yours. Got them black eyes you got. A bitch told me it was sexy once. She said I got sexy eyes, you believe that. They ain't even got a colour they just black... said she could see my soul. What you think about that, man? The jawline and all that shit, ain't it a motherfucker? *(beat)* Why you ain't neva reach down and pick me up? Why you ain't neva pick me up? Well don't stand there

like a fucking mute, you a grown ass man, I'm a grown ass man, let's bump heads, nigga, let's get this shit out. Tell me they beat you down or some shit like that. Tell me you wanted to hear my voice too, you know. Tell me you picked that name for me. Tell me. Tell me you ain't been watching me fall. I swear to God nigga; I swear to God, tell me you ain't push me... I can't do this shit. I can't handle this shit, I ain't strong enough for this. Why you bring me into this world? *(beat)* You damn coward. What you do when they was taking Mom? How you let them take Mommy from me. I ain't got shit in this world, how you let them take Mommy? Nigga you stomped on her soul like she was a piece of shit.

The figure turns his back and starts to walk away.

Don't walk away like a bitch. Be a fuckin man! Be a man and face what you done. You ain't a man, you ain't a man. You ain't shit! Fuck you and fuck your God!!!

The figure turns around to face him. The figure is not his father however, it is now the image of him. JAYQUESE is in a state of confusion. His hands cover his head as he tries to shake the image and the surrounding madness out of his head. He weakly falls to the ground.

The projection fades to black. JAYQUESE lies there helpless, unable to move.

Lights go to black.

Lights come up. It is bright—obviously the next day. JAYQUESE awakens to the brightness. He was almost certain that he had died. He turns around, there is no one. He looks around again, no none. He looks to the ground. Surrounded by cement, no footprints, but he was carried. Calmly he goes into his pocket for his cell phone, and calls TASHA.

Tash... just let me talk, baby. I don't know what's going on, but we can take little steps, little baby steps through it all. I love you, loved you even when I said those things I said. We gonna try and make this work... me you and the baby. Love you.

Something on the ground catches his eye. He reaches out his hand, fully extended, to the ground. He freezes in that position. (The image we are looking for is that of the person sticking their hand into the black hole.) Lights go down, leaving JAYQUESE in silhouette.

Audio: The same as the start. Muffled sound of child saying "Daddy."

Lights go to black.

The end.

Pusha-Man
a.k.a.
The Seed

l to r: David Collins, Mike G-yohannes
photo by Aviva Armour-Ostroff

Pusha-Man a.k.a. The Seed was first produced at Theatre Passe Muraille, Toronto, in October 2005, with the following company:

Benjamin	Mike G-yohannes
Sarah	Cara Ricketts
Absolute	David Collins

Directed by Philip Akin
Stage Managed by Andrea Schurman
Set and Lighting Design by Trevor Schwellnus
Sound Music Coordinator: Nick Murray

CHARACTERS

SARAH: Black female.

BENJAMIN: Black male.

ABSOLUTE: Black, cool as hell, "make my clothes funky, not corny."

PUSHA-MAN
a.k.a.
THE SEED

An ally anywhere. A pregnant Black female (not barefooted) sits on the ground her legs spread wide. Birthing position. She releases a long sustained "Ahhh!!"

SARAH   Ahhh!!!!

The strain of the release is sent throughout the entirety of her body. BENJAMIN walks towards her with two candles in his hands. He is agitated. With each step he takes towards her, he is tempted to break away and run. There is the occasional paranoid look over his back, as if he hears his name called.

BENJAMIN   How are you feeling?

SARAH   I'm scared.

BENJAMIN   You don't have to be scared.

SARAH   You're shaking, you're sweating, how are you going to tell me not to be scared.

BENJAMIN   He's coming. He's gonna be here soon.

SARAH   But I'm feeling all lightheaded, baby. And I can feel my toes getting numb.

BENJAMIN   *(rubs her toes)* Come on Sarah, stay with me. He's gonna come.

SARAH   Well call him! Call out his damn name. Ahh.

BENJAMIN   It don't work like that, it never worked like that before.

SARAH   How did you make me buy into your bullshit.

BENJAMIN   You gotta call him from inside, baby.

SARAH   I'm callin, you don't hear?

BENJAMIN   Please.

SARAH   Ahhhh!!!

BENJAMIN   Hold the candle, Sarah.

SARAH   Ahhh!!!

BENJAMIN tries to have her hold the candle, but she has no strength. She lays there deflated and exhausted. Soldiering on, BENJAMIN picks up both candles. He stands there, eyes closed, as still as his nerves will allow him.

SARAH   Gotta get mellow. *(pause)* Get me mellow now. Pusha-man get me mellow.

Sound cue: "Absolute theme" music.

ABSOLUTE   *(offstage)* I make men wanna fight, and the women wanna lay down at night. *(wink)* What you know about that? I said…

Hearing this, BENJAMIN blows out the candle. The stage is in complete darkness.

(more voiced) Before me there was none, after me none to come. I said what you know about that?

Lights come up on BENJAMIN and SARAH, the other half of the stage is still in darkness. ABSOLUTE enters still in darkness. He walks with a swagger, holding a bottle of Alize.

Poppin collars, Dressed to def, that dapper Don, your Alpha your Omega. Yes homey, your straight up motherfuckin saviour. Your dealer, pushing that rock when they scream. So damn Black, that I'm bright, in the darkness there is light. *(lights come on)* I can be what you need.

SARAH   Gotta be mellow.

ABSOLUTE   What you need?

SARAH   *(tugs on BENJAMIN's pants)* Gotta get me mellow now.

ABSOLUTE   What you really need?

BENJAMIN   Pusha-man get me mellow. *(Bows down before ABSOLUTE's feet. He begins to rub it.)* Eraahh! *(It burns his hands.)* Gotta get us mellow.

ABSOLUTE lifts his hands and then comes down with a heavy slap across BENJAMIN's face causing the stage to brighten. The strike sobers BENJAMIN up.

ABSOLUTE   You seek the comfort of your father's touch?

BENJAMIN   My father's touch? You know there was no comfort in his touch.

ABSOLUTE   But there is comfort in mine.

BENJAMIN   Only you can make me mellow.

SARAH   Ahhh!!

ABSOLUTE   She got you worried?

BENJAMIN   She's pregnant.

ABSOLUTE   Yeh I can see it, I can feel it. *(sniffs)* Smell it.

BENJAMIN   She says it feels like battery acid is in her stomach. It's burning her.

> *ABSOLUTE walks over to SARAH.*

SARAH   *(long sustained)* Ahhh.

ABSOLUTE   Yep, we got a screamer here.

BENJAMIN   You gotta get her mellow.

> *ABSOLUTE holds her hands. She begins to move her pelvis, aroused.*

What's she doing?

> *SARAH begins to orgasm. ABSOLUTE comes down with one mighty slap to her face. Stage brightens. She calms down.*

ABSOLUTE   You have to let it burn, baby, something mighty is in there.

SARAH   This is no child. It's something else in me.

BENJAMIN   I told her you could fix anything.

SARAH   I still don't believe that. Make this burning stop if you can do anything.

ABSOLUTE   You of little faith. *(takes a sip of Alize)* When I say you gotta let it burn, baby, you gotta let it burn.

SARAH   Are you a sicko? Do you get off on pregnant women?

BENJAMIN   Hey, hey, hey, come on now, watch what you say.

ABSOLUTE   Let her talk. Talk to me child. Talk.

SARAH   What can you do for me?

ABSOLUTE   Almost anything you could possibly ask.

SARAH   Why don't you keep me mellow then.

ABSOLUTE   *(shakes his head)* I thought you had more in you.

SARAH   More in me? There is a monster thrashing about my innards. What more do you want from me.

ABSOLUTE   I want some of that two snaps high, two snaps low, neck snapping, I ain't gonna stand for this.

SARAH   I want to feel mellow.

ABSOLUTE   Listen here, I'm not tryna hear nobody use those words again. No mellow, no yellow, no fellow, I don't even wanna hear nothing that sounds like it. Benjamin talk to her.

> *BENJAMIN, noticing ABSOLUTE get irritated, drifts of to the side.*

SARAH   Who are you to levy out rules?

ABSOLUTE   Benjamin.

SARAH   Mellow, I need to be mellow!

ABSOLUTE   Benjamin!!

SARAH   That's all I want. I want to close my eyes and drift. I want cold water to flush through my organs. Get me mellow. *(She repeats "mellow" until it fades off.)*

> *ABSOLUTE raises his hand as if to come down with a mighty blow on her. He keeps his hand suspended in the air. Looks over to see BENJAMIN rocking on the ground. ABSOLUTE swaggers over to BENJAMIN.*

ABSOLUTE   Speak, son, on the real what's the deal.

BENJAMIN   Evil thoughts reside within me, and I'm not seeking absolution. I wanted you to come down with the wrath of countless woes. I wanted both the earth and the heavens to shake. I wanted you to strike her until she was no more.

ABSOLUTE   Son.

BENJAMIN   Pusha-man, I know it seems like cowardice but I can't father this child. I've never wanted to father this child. I do not have love for this woman.

ABSOLUTE   Remember a time you called me from deep inside. "Pusher man, pusher man. Gotta get me mellow now." You were all strung out, your head shaved clean absent of a single follicle.

BENJAMIN   I'm just an ordinary child, dreaming of being an ordinary man.

ABSOLUTE   You said you were so alone. I offered you love or lust.

BENJAMIN   Why even offer me a choice. I'm a retard, I've been a retard all my life. Why offer me a choice.

ABSOLUTE   The child was always gonna be, it was a choice of love or lust.

BENJAMIN   You neva told me that. No. I was alone but I didn't want to love. To love some woman, to have her filled with expectations; only for her to see I wasn't strong enough for her. That I couldn't even provide for myself. Can you see me just endlessly disappointing someone? Having every day to live with my own shortcomings. No. I just wanted to get mellow. I just wanted a sweet hit. I wanted lust to keep me moving. There is no moving with a woman holding you back.

ABSOLUTE   So I should strike her?

BENJAMIN   I don't even think it's my child.

ABSOLUTE   So I should strike her?

BENJAMIN   Is it even possible, that it's mine?

ABSOLUTE   Word is she was a virgin before you cut through.

BENJAMIN   I know, and it's true. She bled that time, that one and only time.

ABSOLUTE   So what is the problem?

BENJAMIN   That time…

ABSOLUTE   What about that time?

BENJAMIN   While we were having sex.

ABSOLUTE   Yes while you were hitting the bone, what?

BENJAMIN   I looked down and saw her blood. And all of a sudden I felt horrible about what I was doing. I knew the pretense was false, I knew I was stealing something from her. But with each stroke after that, I was losing my erection.

ABSOLUTE   The spirit wasn't willing so the flesh became weak.

BENJAMIN   Maybe it was the guilt or the stress. Pusha-man, I couldn't just go soft on her. I couldn't screw up again. So I just started pounding her faster and acted like I came. But I didn't, I pulled out and went to the bathroom. It was her first time right, so I'm hoping she wouldn't know. I'm holding myself *(penis)* in my hands all turtled when out of nowhere she starts moaning. But it's not the moaning like I was hearing when I was with her. It was different, it was like its own language. The last thing I remember is lambasting myself cause she was making herself feel better than I was making her feel. Next day she pregnant. But I never came Pusha. I never came.

ABSOLUTE   You had the lights all dimmed, saving yourself from her judging the size of that Black rod of yours. Just enough light for you to see the blood. Mang *(man)* I done been saying, "in the darkness there is light."

BENJAMIN   Pusha, Pusha, it was her choice to take the lights off, I'm not ashamed of my body. But it was her first time you understand. She was nervous she was self conscious.

ABSOLUTE   Did you try and put her at ease?

BENJAMIN   I gave her a soft kiss, held her hands, and told her it wouldn't hurt. I bit her ear and whispered it would be pleasurable.

ABSOLUTE   And her hopes rejoiced. Her heart danced, her breasts were swole.

BENJAMIN   I never wanted to hurt her.

ABSOLUTE   You felt alive, and she felt alive. And the joy of the flesh was an intoxicating one.

BENJAMIN   I never wanted to hurt her.

ABSOLUTE   It's beautiful to partake in the flesh.

BENJAMIN   I would take it all back.

ABSOLUTE   You were gentle with her. Though lust was your spark, it was with love that you handled her—

BENJAMIN   Maybe love of the flesh, but I was all wrong—

ABSOLUTE   As long as I've know you, you've been a creature of regrets.

BENJAMIN   As long as I've known you, you've always led me astray. Every time I get a hit I think I'm getting better. But all I want is another hit.

ABSOLUTE   Ease up. Dat nah mek it. Blouse and skirts, pants and shirt. Dat nah mek it. Do you not love me?

BENJAMIN   I'd be a fool to answer.

ABSOLUTE   These mighty fists are going in my pocket. Answer.

BENJAMIN   They staying there?

ABSOLUTE   These mighty fists are going in my pocket, and they are staying in there.

BENJAMIN   Is fear the same thing as love?

ABSOLUTE   They never been brothers, even if they sit at the same table.

BENJAMIN   Pusha, I cower in your presence. I am submissive to you. I fear your right hand as much as your left. Cause if Pusha-man ever leaves, what's gonna get me over? How am I gonna get mellow?

ABSOLUTE   You make my heart cry. Tears shall fall where they never fell.

BENJAMIN   Pusha, Pusha, Pusha, I'm sorry. I never wanted to hurt you. I would take it all back.

ABSOLUTE   Are you sorry cause you think I'm hurt, or are you sorry because you fear I'll take my shit and leave?

BENJAMIN   Because of love.

ABSOLUTE   It's futile to lie in the face of truth. You should not let your tongue betray your heart. That deception wears itself like a spring jacket in the harshest months of winter.

BENJAMIN   Well why the fists of fury? Why the pimp slapping? Why the, "into the darkness; in that place there will be weeping and gnashing of teeth"? Where is the love in that?

ABSOLUTE   (*strikes a pose, one hand extended high, his slap pose*) Look at this. Tell me this ain't straight gangsta. That mighty slap, son that was just some dramatic flare. I got nice body lines that's all. The truth is I could sneeze on you and have the same effect. Forget sneeze, that's kinda unsanitary; I could just blink.

BENJAMIN   Then I wouldn't fear your right hand, but I would fear your eye.

ABSOLUTE   Benjamin I do not want you to fear me. But I want you to respect me. Respect my might. Respect my right hand. Respect the swagger, the dip in my walk. Respect *moi.*

BENJAMIN   Or else?

ABSOLUTE   Or else I'll rain down on you like falling rocks of Mount Zion. Come upside your head with thunder and lightening. *(pause)* I'm pulling your G-string mang.

BENJAMIN   Or else, answer me that.

ABSOLUTE   Or else you fail to understand me. You fail to understand what it is I want from you. You fail to see who you are.

BENJAMIN   I am and have always been a failure.

ABSOLUTE   Your true impact is yet to be felt by this world.

BENJAMIN   Don't you get it; I don't want to have an impact.

ABSOLUTE   You don't have a say in that.

BENJAMIN   I've never had a say. When was my voice ever heard?

ABSOLUTE   When was your voice ever heard? *(pause)* I may have made a mistake with you. I might be answering the wrong doorbell. *(begins to walk)*

BENJAMIN   Pusha.

ABSOLUTE   Someone else is calling me.

BENJAMIN   What about her?

ABSOLUTE   The pain will cease.

BENJAMIN   The baby?

ABSOLUTE   It will also cease.

BENJAMIN   But you said it was always going to be.

ABSOLUTE   Yes it is, just not for you.

BENJAMIN   Don't punish me. *(picks up the left behind bottle of Alize)*

ABSOLUTE   You're punishing yourself.

BENJAMIN   Sorry, all I needed was to get mellow.

ABSOLUTE   Quit with that mellow— *(turns around, sees the bottle)* Put that down.

BENJAMIN   *(opens it)* Once I'm mellow we can talk.

ABSOLUTE   Put that down, Benjamin.

BENJAMIN   Getting mellow for you Pusha. Getting mellow. *(drinks)*

    Bright spotlight on BENJAMIN.

ABSOLUTE   That's some holy spirit up in there, boy, that too strong for you.

BENJAMIN   Oh, man you been keeping this away from me. This is crunk.

ABSOLUTE   Go on, go on then.

BENJAMIN   Eh, Pusha I got wings on me. You see them, you see my wings? *(jumps up and down)*

ABSOLUTE   Benjamin that's enough now.

BENJAMIN   But I got wings. I'll be damned.

ABSOLUTE   Keep drinking and you will be.

BENJAMIN   *(uncontrollable laughter)* Who's tickling my balls. Who's tickling my balls. I'm tea-bagging baby, I'm tea-bagging.

ABSOLUTE   The ride down will be heavy, Benjamin.

BENJAMIN   Then I'll drink more.

ABSOLUTE   That won't help. In the light there is darkness.

BENJAMIN   No time for that Pusha, just time for… Pusha…

ABSOLUTE   Yes, son.

BENJAMIN   I can see right through you.

ABSOLUTE   Come back to me, I will help you.

    The spot begins to fade.

BENJAMIN   *(screams)* Ahhh. *(pause)* My mouth's dry. My mouth is dry. *(Spotlight is gone, he faints.)*

    ABSOLUTE gathers him up to his feet. BENJAMIN is standing but completely out of body. ABSOLUTE undoes the buttons to his shirt.

ABSOLUTE   My breasts are full. Drink. "Whoever drinks of my water shall never thirst. But the water that I will give him will become in him a well of water springing up to eternal life." *(He lays BENJAMIN back to the ground.)* Let it work, baby, let it work. It take you out like bush rum ehh.

    ABSOLUTE walks around hands extended wide. He starts jamming, getting into some calypso.

Oouudey, ouuudey ohh. Ouuudey, oouuuudey ohhh
I drop a seed in a piece ah land
Seed sprung up and ah called it man
Who woulda know that this creation
Would need so much blasted attention.
Oouudey, ouuudey ohh. Ouuudey, oouuuudey ohhh
Outta the darkness there came light
Light him enamoured by his own might
Darkness forget he the one come first
Living he life like a dirty curse.
Oouudey, ouuudey ohh. Ouuudey, oouuuudey ohhh
Land vex that he spit up the seed
He say man ain't nothing but a destructive weed
Look at how long you give them a chance
Bout time you leggo some pestilence
Ehhh, ehhh, is that he say?
Like he's the real man, forget about meh.
Oouudey, ouuudey ohh. If they only know
Land huff and puff till he belly rumbling
So much commotion he ain't hear she belly mumbling
Look—
Yuh eye'in me down like I should do something
Is blind yuh blind, yuh can't see that I woking *(working)*
Hear she nahh—Is wok that I woking
In the belly of she ocean is the start of something…

SARAH   Ahhhh…

> *ABSOLUTE moves towards her.*

ABSOLUTE   If you hear the ocean mumbling.

SARAH   Benjamin?

> *ABSOLUTE holds her scalp then lets his hands work through her hair.*

ABSOLUTE   A sweet child, Sarah. So much strength you don't know about.

> *He brings her to her feet. She is in a comatose state, not really functionally there. ABSOLUTE runs his hands up and down her arms.*

So soft. So very soft.

> *He goes behind her, wrapping his arms around her body, his hands on her belly.*

SARAH   Ummmm ahhh…

> *A slow moan is released. He sways side to side with her. This causes her moan to build. It is the most beautiful sound. The sound of angels singing.*

ABSOLUTE *(as they sway)* "Whoever drinks of my water shall never thirst. But the water that I will give him will become in him a well of water springing up to eternal life."

SARAH Ummm ahhh…

ABSOLUTE Yes, yes.

SARAH Ummmm…

> *With one hand on her belly, ABSOLUTE runs the other down her thighs. This excites her, causing a seamless switch between notes.*

ABSOLUTE There is something mighty in you.

> *A bewildered BENJAMIN awakens. He tries to grasp what is happening. But that moan, that moan hits him hard.*

BENJAMIN That's it! That is the moan! It was you?

> *BENJAMIN, enraged, goes after ABSOLUTE. Ripping him away from SARAH. He starts pounding on him. Without ABSOLUTE's touch, SARAH falls to the ground.*

You lay your hands on her after me??

ABSOLUTE Take it easy, son.

BENJAMIN You felt the need to finish what I started? You felt the need to belittle me?

ABSOLUTE It's deeper than that, Benjamin.

BENJAMIN I am a man!

ABSOLUTE I know.

BENJAMIN No matter how many times in my life I acted like a bitch, I am a man!

ABSOLUTE That you are.

BENJAMIN Shut up! *(slaps him)*

ABSOLUTE Hit me again.

> *BENJAMIN hits him.*

And again.

> *BENJAMIN complies.*

That's the most fire I've ever seen from you, Benjamin. It's about time.

BENJAMIN   How could you betray me like this?

ABSOLUTE   Are you angry?

BENJAMIN   Of course, of course I'm angry. What does this look like to you?

ABSOLUTE   Remember this feeling. Remember what it took to fight back. You know I could obliterate you with a wink; but you said enough is enough and you fought back.

BENJAMIN   What, you teaching me a lesson? Nahhh that's bullshit! This ain't funny, this ain't no class.

ABSOLUTE   No it's not funny! None of this shit been funny!! A multitude of you waking my ass up on a Sunday morning, when I'm spose to be at rest so that I can make you mellow, that shit for sure ain't funny. It ain't funny no matter how many hallelujahs you spit. Your poor asses dropping your last 5 dollars into a plate that I ain't never going to see, that ain't funny. Got damn it buy some food! But you know what's really not funny? I come to you in the ally, I'm your Pusha-man, I can push you what you need, what's good for your soul. But you don't ask for the strength to stand up and fight for your manhood. For your piece of the pie. All your Black asses ever want is for me to sedate your mind. Disenfranchised souls, belittled and suppressed; and not one collective force to bring balance back into this world. Now, my son, that shit ain't motherfuckin funny. *(pause)*

BENJAMIN   *(deliberate)* I ain't said hallelujah in 5 years. So I know you not talking about me. You not throwing Tom, Dick and Mary's blame on my back. You not going to use all that bullshit to justify what you did. I ain't the sharpest pencil, but all that verbage don't cleanse you.

ABSOLUTE   It's a bigger issue than you.

BENJAMIN   No such thing. You can't horn me, you can't horn me and then try to rationalize it. You don't take another man's woman and tell him it was for a "bigger issue."

ABSOLUTE   Son—

BENJAMIN   Don't son me. A father would never lay with his son's woman. He doesn't double dip. You betrayed me in the dark. You all hard and erect, and I'm looking in the mirror with my dick all turtled. She's singing out for you and I'm all in knots listening to her. That's just sick. That's just disgusting.

ABSOLUTE   Sometimes the son can't do the father's job. They don't know how to hold them. They don't know where to touch.

BENJAMIN   Father's touch? I don't know how to hold them? *(pause)* I don't. I don't. But you already knew this. Hundreds of nights I opened up my soul to you. I said, "Pusha, I don't know what they want." I said, "Pusha, I don't know what to give them."

ABSOLUTE   "Pusha, how do I make her cum?" That's your favourite one. "Pusha, I have to make sure she cums, how do I make her cum."

BENJAMIN   Yeh, sometimes I asked that a lot.

ABSOLUTE   And what did I tell you?

BENJAMIN   You said, "put it out your mind Benjamin, you worry too much, just hold her."

ABSOLUTE   Spoken like a pimp.

BENJAMIN   It was all lies. A big set-up. Leave me all inadequate and then just slide in and finish it all up. Geeze, she was probably grateful. Was she? Was she grateful?

ABSOLUTE   You're always asking me the wrong questions.

BENJAMIN   Did she laugh at me?

ABSOLUTE   Wrong questions.

> *BENJAMIN looks over at SARAH, then at ABSOLUTE.*

BENJAMIN   How do you respect a whore?

ABSOLUTE   She's no whore.

BENJAMIN   A woman don't make those types of sounds unless she's liking it.

ABSOLUTE   She's an innocent party to this.

BENJAMIN   A woman don't make those types of sounds unless she's liking it!

ABSOLUTE   That's an interesting way to look at it. If she gives it up to me and likes it, she's a whore. If she gives it up to me and doesn't like it, she's not a whore. But what if I didn't like it Benjamin?

BENJAMIN   She was a pity lay, Pusha? You mean to tell me you came around with your water truck *(sexual reference)* outta pity? You felt so sorry for her Black ass that you had to give her some Pusha juice—

ABSOLUTE   It's higher mathematics.

BENJAMIN   I wonder how she'd feel knowing it was some pity screw.

> *BENJAMIN walks over to SARAH. Begins to shake her.*

How would she feel.

ABSOLUTE   Leave her alone.

BENJAMIN   *(shakes)* How would she feel.

ABSOLUTE   Leave her alone

BENJAMIN   *(shakes her)* Sarah, I got some big news.

ABSOLUTE   The men are talking!! *(pause)* If I wanted her to hear this she'd hear it.

BENJAMIN   Well it ain't up to you no more.

ABSOLUTE   Don't get ahead of yourself, you don't wanna leave your shadow behind.

BENJAMIN   You gonna drop some wrath on me now? Go ahead, I'm as good as dead. I got horns on my head, I ain't a man.

ABSOLUTE   *(calypso)* Ouudey, Oudey ohhh, oudey, ouudey ohh.
Who woulda know that this creation
Woulda cause so much blasted confusion
I shoulda see it comin, I didn't see it at all
I shoulda see it comin, I didn't see it at all

BENJAMIN   No noise.

ABSOLUTE   If my two eye was open
I woulda see the tables turn
But no, no, I rest it for awhile
Now, he go re-enact everything that he know
And pestilence on my body he'll throw

BENJAMIN   Shut up.

ABSOLUTE   I don't blame him for wanting to wear daddy jockey shorts
But it too big so he whole asshole go get exposed of course

BENJAMIN   You loud—

ABSOLUTE   He whole asshole go get exposed!!

> *BENJAMIN grabs him.*

Of course.

> *BENJAMIN takes ABSOLUTE's belt and ties his extended hands to a lightpost. He takes off ABSOLUTE's pants, and then ties his legs to the light post with a plastic bag on the ground. ABSOLUTE does not fight back. We see ABSOLUTE in a semi crucifix position. BENJAMIN, puts on ABSOLUTE's pants, tries to get his power. He steps back, then runs towards ABSOLUTE hitting him in the gut.*

BENJAMIN   Where is the wrath! *(runs at him again)*

> *ABSOLUTE does nothing.*

(runs at him again) Do something.

> *Dejected BENJAMIN makes his way to SARAH. Throughout this he is conscious of keeping the pants from falling off his ass.*

Do you hear me? *(no response)* Hey, hey, Sarah wake up. *(He touches his fingers to her lips. Longing for a reaction he lays with her, dry-humping her as he holds her.)* Sing for me. *(Silence. He gets up and drags her body before ABSOLUTE.)*

> *BENJAMIN hovering over SARAH, his hands in the PUSHA slap pose.*

What would you do, Absolute? How would you rectify the situation? Should I strike her?

SARAH   *(barely audible)* Benjamin…

BENJAMIN   Should I strike her?

SARAH   *(whimper)* Ahh…

BENJAMIN   What is just?

> *SARAH awakens. She weakly looks up to see BENJAMIN looking down on her in the PUSHA pose.*

SARAH   What are you doing?

BENJAMIN   I'm thinking about how justified I am to strike you.

SARAH   Why would you strike me?

BENJAMIN   Because you let him… do things to you.

SARAH   Who? What things?

BENJAMIN   No, no, no, *(He loses it.)* no, no. no. no. no. no. you know, you know what he did.

SARAH   I don't.

BENJAMIN   You know, you know, you know what he did. *(cries)* I heard you I heard the whole thing. No, no, no.

SARAH   Stop, please stop.

BENJAMIN   Just lies, Sarah. It's all lies. There is no high there is no cure. It's all lies, ahhh.

SARAH   Don't say that. Call your friend.

> *BENJAMIN holds her head towards ABSOLUTE.*

BENJAMIN   He's a lie.

SARAH   But you said he could do anything.

BENJAMIN   Look at him. He didn't even fight back. He made me think he was more than he really is. He didn't even fight back.

SARAH   Call him, Benjamin. *(She tries to undo the plastic bag.)*

BENJAMIN   He didn't fight back. He's all lies. There is no truth.

Lights go to black. Pause.

ABSOLUTE   Let the truth be seen.

Spotlight comes up on ABSOLUTE. ABSOLUTE is magically freed from the ties.

(to BENJAMIN) That passive shit really can get to you, can't it. *(breaks into laughter)* He wants to know the truth! Running around like a madman, cause he wants to know the truth. Then ask me, ask me for the "truth."

BENJAMIN   What is the truth?

Full lights come on. BENJAMIN and SARAH facing ABSOLUTE. Showdown.

ABSOLUTE   I'll tell you the truth, but you gotta give me my pants. My draws ain't as white as I thought they were.

BENJAMIN takes off ABSOLUTE's pants and throws them to him.

Sleep, child. *(SARAH falls to the ground. ABSOLUTE puts on his pants.)* You calmed down some? *(pause)* Your heart beating mighty fast ain't it?

BENJAMIN   Yes, sir.

ABSOLUTE   You still pissed at me. But you happy I do exist.

BENJAMIN   Yes, sir.

ABSOLUTE   The truth is a difficult thing to grasp. It opens your mind to areas with no boundaries. It can be a most unsafe feeling, the truth.

BENJAMIN   When I didn't believe in you, I felt liberated from you. I had to defend myself.

ABSOLUTE   How did that feel?

BENJAMIN   Powerful, but scary.

ABSOLUTE   Grab your balls, Benjamin. *(He does so.)* I bet they never felt as full or as heavy.

BENJAMIN   I never felt them.

ABSOLUTE   The balls are quite something. They're in the middle of the body just hanging there. Keeping you grounded, keeping you centred. Every now and then you need to just grab them. Just grab them and say "yeah." Make your face all nasty and say, "yeahh."

BENJAMIN   *(grabs his balls)* Did you sleep with her?

ABSOLUTE   Ohh, the complications of the truth… in the literal sense I could never have sex with her.

BENJAMIN   But I heard her.

ABSOLUTE   You said you wanted to hear the truth. In the literal sense I could never have sex with her.

BENJAMIN   But the sounds, the way you touched her, the baby?

ABSOLUTE   It opens your mind to areas with no boundaries, that silly thing the truth. No sex. You believe me don't you? *(pause)*

BENJAMIN   Yes.

ABSOLUTE   Your impulse is to fight against it, but you believe me. Why is that?

BENJAMIN   Because it sounds different.

ABSOLUTE   *(laughs)* It does, it has its own sound. It's an odd relationship, the one between balls and ears. *(laughs)*

BENJAMIN   Pusha. *(smiles)*

ABSOLUTE   I put you through a lot tonight. Toyed with your emotions. And you fought through it without a hit. You felt an injustice and you held me accountable, without a hit. Thought you wupped my ass, without a hit. Sidebar, I let you get away with that. You can call me, and I will come, but it will not be to give you a hit. I'll help you discover the truth, but I won't let you mask it.

BENJAMIN   Why go through all this with me?

ABSOLUTE   It's the seed that's been buried by stones, that will truly appreciate the sun.

BENJAMIN   *(points to SARAH)* And her?

ABSOLUTE   Sun's not enough, seed needs water.

BENJAMIN   And the child?

ABSOLUTE   I just answered you. Think it through. *(pause)* Benjamin it's yours. There is a revolutionary darkness in that belly. With the spirit and the fire to bring about balance. And I leave it to you to nurture and father. And when you hold that child make sure it is a touch of comfort, it'll need that.

BENJAMIN   How do I get her through this?

ABSOLUTE   Give her a soft kiss, hold her hands and tell her you'll never hurt her. Bite her ear and whisper your lives will be pleasurable. Grab your balls, tell her, "no mellow, let it burn." That Benjamin is the mother of change. It is within her torment and pain that the child will gain strength; love her.

BENJAMIN   You believe in me like that? *(still holding balls)*

ABSOLUTE   You dropped the comatose behaviour, Benjamin. You ready to truly live now. There is no turning back. You like the feeling of those balls don't you?

BENJAMIN   Yes.

ABSOLUTE   Then I believe in you.

BENJAMIN   Are you leaving me now?

ABSOLUTE   You know how to reach me. *(picks up Alize)* And I ain't leaving this for you. That tea-bagging was a bit tooo much. *(starts his swagger)*

BENJAMIN   Pusha.

ABSOLUTE   What's that.

BENJAMIN   One last time lemme see that pose.

ABSOLUTE   *(laughs)* Yeh, alright. *(strikes his mighty slap pose)*

BENJAMIN   Mang you do have nice body lines. *(smirks)*

ABSOLUTE   Sho nufff! Gotta get a move on, there's a woman calling for some Pusha, Pusha right about now.

> As ABSOLUTE *starts to swagger off, the lights on his side of the stage starts to fade.*

Momentary distraction, or a lasting impression?
Weighed down by history, or freed of such burdens?
Questions, questions, can the darkness last.
Whoo-hoooo,… *(He exits.)*

> BENJAMIN *takes a moment to himself, then goes over to SARAH.*

BENJAMIN   *(kisses her, holds her hands)* I will never hurt you. *(bites her ear)* I promise our lives will be pleasurable.

> SARAH *begins to come out of her comatose state.*

SARAH   Benjamin?

BENJAMIN   I'm right here, Sarah.

SARAH   Is he coming, Benjamin, is your friend coming?

BENJAMIN   Not right now Sarah, but he'll come soon enough.

SARAH   You said he'd come, I trusted you.

BENJAMIN   I'm here for you, Sarah.

SARAH   But I can't take this. It's burning. I need to get mel—

BENJAMIN   *(covers her mouth) No,* no you don't. Let it burn, baby, let it burn, there is something mighty in you.

SARAH   *(loud sustained)* AHHH!!

       Lights fade to black.

       The end.

Trinidadian born. Scarborough raised (Canada). Joseph is a York University graduate with a BFA in Acting. His first works were independently produced projects. *Born Ready* and *Pusha-Man* marked his mainstream introduction to the Toronto Theatre Scene. His goal as a writer has always been to inject the life experiences and culture around him into his work. To reflect the images and struggles of a people that rarely see themselves on stage, yet whose stories are as valued as any other.